Slow Lane

THE BEAUTIFUL ART OF SLOWING DOWN

MONICA WILKINSON

SLOW LANE
THE BEAUTIFUL ART OF SLOWING DOWN

Published by:
NyreePress Literary Group
Fort Worth, TX
www.nyreepress.com
contact@nyreepress.com

ISBN print: 978-1-945304-06-4
Library of Congress Control Catalog-in-Data Number: in process

Categories:
1. CHRISTIAN LIVING / 2. Inspirational

Printed in the United States of America on acid free paper

nyreepress

Dedicated to:

For all the loves who share my home and heart: Emily, Rachel, Samuel and David. You are the reasons I want to slow and enjoy every moment of this life God has richly blessed me with. I am beyond grateful for the privilege of being wife and mama alongside you four. I love you.

For my parents who have modeled the beautiful side of slow for many years. You are walking a hard road with a slow not chosen but you are still modeling the beauty in it despite the struggle. You are brave. You are courageous. By God's grace, you are both survivors. I love you.

CONTENTS

Note: Why the NIV version of the Bible? I know we all have versions of the Bible we love for very specific and good reasons. I have chosen to use the NIV simply because it best suited my study needs and familiarity in finding passages in my NIV Study Bible. I hope you will freely pick up your own version as you work through this hands-on book and enjoy the translation you are most familiar and comfortable with.

INTRODUCTION

Dear Friend,

Thank you for picking up a copy of this book! My dearest hope and prayer for you is that you will meet God deeply in these pages. The format for this book is different than most, allow me to walk you through it for a moment.

The first part of this book will read as a typical non-fiction book with some journaling questions provided for you to process as you are learning and moving through. As you proceed, you will want to have a Bible handy for looking up verses and digging into your own personal study.

There are lots of opportunities for you to journal and respond to the ideas presented throughout this book. I like to think of this as a handbook of sorts for slowing down. It is a process and a journey, one which I hope to be able to guide you through during these pages as I have walked through these things in my own life.

By the time you reach Part Four, you will be in a full fledged Bible Study of your own that you can work through in your own personal study time.

There are several Appendices at the back of this book which I trust will be helpful to you. I especially want to mention that there is an art print you can remove from the book and display in your home or tuck into your Bible to remind you of the things you are learning. A set of verse cards can also be removed and you will find more about how to use these in Part Three as we look at Slowing Stress.

You may want to read through the book once and then go back through a second time to linger over sections that have journaling questions or Bible study for you to complete.

However you choose to use this, may God receive all the glory for anything good and beneficial you find here.

Learning to slow along with you,

Monica

PART ONE
Pull Over

Fast Lane

"Dear Lord, I have failed again. I started my day with You and then the tension and pressure started to creep in. By breakfast I thought I might explode or completely fall apart. {deep breath} I need You, God."

Can you relate? Life is busy, and not all of it is within our control. Despite our best efforts to avoid over-scheduling, sometimes things just happen that way. We are all busy and life is really full.

Yet, I have to ask: why are we throwing our lot in with crazy busy and living like it is OKAY? And even more, what is the price we are paying for living like this? What message are we sending those around us? Our spouses? Our children?

The prayer above was very real and describes my morning. I knelt down in my bedroom before a busy day and begged God for His help.

I still get over-scheduled sometimes and find myself hurrying and running late and regretting the choices that got me into the situation I'm facing. I get overwhelmed in heart and mind, and that is not a slow attitude.

Even though our family has made deliberate efforts to slow, life still creeps in and sweeps us along with the current. I want to convey this right up front: I am not perfect. I have failed today at resisting the effects of the pressure and stress of what needs to be done and the expectations {real and imagined} that come with it. I am a real woman, wife, mom, daughter, sister, and friend living in the same world as you.

Monica Wilkinson

But, here's the thing – I'm not at peace with the crazy of busy on a regular basis. It does a number on my heart and body that leaves me feeling like a wrung-out dishrag. Sweet friend, I believe with all my heart this is not the way our God wants us to move through the lives He has blessed us with.

Even my feeble and small efforts at slowing have been blessed and a blessing. It stirs up a yearning to ask, seek, and knock on the door of slowing. I want God to take my hand and lead me in the lessons of slow, to be my perfect teacher and gentle Shepherd.

I humbly submit to you that the hand holding this pen and typing on this laptop is not an expert. What I do have is a student's heart to keep at this journey of slow and a burden to share it with you, trusting that God will use it by His grace and for His glory.

If you are left limp by the pace of life, this book is for you. It's also for your family, those around you, and most of all, your soul.

Slow Start

Every summer, I take a day retreat by myself. One day to reflect, pray, and seek God for the coming school year and routine for our family. This is where my slow journey began – I was sitting on a castle terrace with a trickling fountain nearby and the gorgeous, blue, Colorado sky overhead on a clear summer day. Thinking ahead to the beginning of a new year of homeschooling our children and getting back into our normal routine, my heart was beating faster, and I was feeling overwhelmed before it even began.

Bringing this to prayer and really seeking God began my journey through intentional slowing. More than a year after the above day retreat and with a new year quickly arriving, God was again laying this word *slow* on my heart and mind. I named it my "word for the year" and steeped myself in processing this idea and lifestyle.

These pages are born out of living, reflecting, processing, studying, failing, and picking back up again in slowing. Here in this space, I will share from the overflow of *slow* in our home and in my heart. This collection of thoughts will be part Bible study and part journal, with reflections and musings from my journey thrown in. I hope as you walk through this gathering of thoughts and photos, it will be a deep sigh of peace, stillness, and yes, slow.

My goals in slowing are to be able to enjoy the beauty of everyday moments added up together to create a treasure of memories, a lifetime of legacy, and an investment in my own children, home, and family that is not rushed. I want us to have time to examine a flower, watch a bird eating seeds at the bird feeder at our front window, run outside, and drive quickly to the boat landing to chase a sunset. I will never regret one day that I enjoyed one of these moments, but you can be sure I would be full of regret if I missed them.

Like so many things, it can be overwhelming to consider a lifestyle change. It's kind of like making a decision to change your eating habits. First, you are aware and you have a desire to make a change. You may start learning about different foods and why you want to eliminate them or increase them based on what you learn. You may start reading labels, looking at food sources, making more from scratch, etc… but do you do this all at once? Perhaps. Many of us, however, would choose one piece of that at a time to tackle and let it build slowly.

Making the decision to deliberately choose a slower lifestyle can be like that, which is why in this book I propose the idea of a patchwork of slow ideas. See each of the ideas or thoughts presented as one square of a quilt. Start on one square, and pretty soon you may decide to add another square and another. Stitched together, these humble ideas will make a beautiful piece of art and will create a beautiful life of slowing.

However, do not feel discouraged if you only choose one "square" to bring to your life and implement. If you choose to slow in one way, it will still be a beautiful blessing in your life and home.

Slow Journal

Where are you in your slow journey? Just starting? Well along the path?

—the beginning

If there is a stirring in your heart to slow, describe particulars of how you want and/or need to slow. What is your vision for slowing?

to have time to get things done and the peace to do it willingly

What does slow mean to you?

To trust God with my time.

Read Psalm 23. How does it invite slowness to your heart and soul? How can you allow God to be your Shepherd today? Picture yourself in these verses and imagine the slowing.

Lay down in green pastures.
I would normally be to worried to do that

Look at Psalm 46:10. How does this verse invoke slowing to you?

Two Kinds of Slow

Before we go on, I think it is important to mention that when I talk about slow, it means more than one thing. I am focusing on two kinds of slow in this book: 1) a heart posture before God and 2) a physical slowing in how we enjoy little moments of everyday life. Sometimes I struggle to clearly communicate what is in my heart about slow and how to describe it to someone else. Here are a few thoughts that come to mind in how I think of slow:

- Savor simple moments

- Be still; take time to just "be" instead of always "do"

- Recognize that slow can be for both for your heart and mind

Remember, we will still fail, over-commit, run late, forget important things, and possibly bark out orders. Sometimes we will still choose productivity and fast instead of slow and savor. And I know you are already thinking, *When do I get anything done if I am slowing?* We're getting to that. Hang in there and know that I am learning right alongside you.

When I first chose *slow* for my word of the year, I searched for books about slowing. I wanted to know more and dig into this idea. There are titles available that fit what I was looking for, but as I began to read and look deeper, I didn't finish a single one because there was something big missing: God.

I wanted to know where God was in slow, and I did not find it in a book from a bookstore. Instead, I got out my Bible and began searching for myself. Many of the Slow Journal entries and Bible Study portions included in this book are from that journey of searching for God in slow. Slow has become a way of life for me, a passion and a huge part of my home and family. I hope that by sharing these thoughts with you, you will find encouragement to step out of the frantic and into the quiet slow. Most of all, I hope you will be closer to God when you reach the back cover by spending time in His Word, looking into your heart, talking to Him, and just considering how to worship Him in the everyday moments of life.

Happy Mail

A quick walk to your mailbox reveals a handwritten envelope with your name on it; it's the best kind of mail! A card or invitation waiting just for you! God has sent us our own set of Happy Mail letters wrapped up in the pages of His Word.

Fun mail says ...

You are known.

You are loved.

You are wanted.

You are included.

You are invited.

I want you on this journey of slow with me. There is strength in numbers and great encouragement in traveling with linked arms. It feels like most of the world around us is swirling faster and faster all the time. Let's step out of the swirling vortex and just stop. Let's refuse to make crazy busy and uptight our norm. Let's slow down *together*.

An Invitation

Breathe deep.

Let it out slowly.

Imagine you are on a bustling highway in a sleek, speedy car. Traffic is cutting in and out all around you as everyone is in a hurry for some reason or another.

Now imagine trading that in for the family car on a winding, scenic country road. There are trees lining one side and a beautiful open meadow on the other.

Since you are reading this, I can only assume that you prefer the second scenario—enjoying nature's beauty while being able to take the scenic route and slowing down.

Our culture wraps up a jam-packed schedule and frantic pace and sets it on a silver platter, offering it like a trophy to anyone who wants it.

But I propose we take that glittery package back and exchange it for a less traveled road, one that celebrates and enjoys the precious, everyday moments of life.

Let's move into the *slow lane* and unwrap the gifts the Giver of Life bestows on us every day.

Won't you join me in slowing?

PART II
A Slow Heart

Understanding Slow

"Vacation has a way of slowing us down – in all its headiness. And the peace it brings gives me reason to pause and consider how I can bottle this slowness and bring it home. I don't mean we've been laying around and doing nothing – we've had lots of fun. It is more of a mental slowness and yes, even the physical slowness."

I wrote these words in the summer of 2012 after we had made our annual jaunt to my parents' home in Colorado. I love going for an extended period of time in the summer, as it really is a true slowing.

So what does it mean to slow down? What is slowing?

First, let's start with what it isn't. Slow is not laziness. It is not an aversion to work or productivity. Slow is not an excuse and, like a lot of things, we must learn to balance slow.

I think slow is choosing to live at a less frantic pace. Choosing peace over hurry and a deep breath over stress. Slow is embracing everyday beauty and taking the time to enjoy it. Hurry rushes by this beauty and misses it, becoming all the poorer for the moments missed.

To me, slow is a quietness of heart and spirit that is focused on God and on what He desires for our days.

If you look up the word *slow* in the dictionary, you will find several negative connotations for this word. Isn't that how the world is, though? Taking something beautiful and making it less desirable

and even ugly to us. At the beginning of my slow journey, I was determined to search the Bible and find the blessings in slow. I pray that God will open your heart and mind to seeking slow in His Word and the world around you.

One thing God brought to mind is an acronym that embodies what slow means to me. Let's explore …

Surrender

Surrender is a hard word and concept to swallow, mainly because it involves giving something up or even more than one something.

The sign language for this word illustrates beautifully and even physically this letting go of one thing and having open hands for what is better. There are varying options found on the web, but the way I learned is to hold your hands as if you are holding a bucket at each side of your body. Then, drop the buckets and bring your hands around and up so your palms are facing up, open towards Heaven.

As I've pondered slow, one word that has consistently come to mind is surrender. Slow is a posture of surrendering: have you noticed that when you are in a hurry, it creates stress? This posture of surrender agrees to choose God's way, realize we may not get everything done we think we must get done, and choose a more manageable pace that will bring a calmer peace rather than a frantic haste.

For me, hurry/feeling rushed is one of the quickest ways to stress. It is one reason I love to work ahead and even make myself plan ahead more and more – the more I have prepared ahead, the more smoothly the transitions go.

Surrender.

Everything does not have to be perfect.

Everything does not have to be finished right this minute.

Remember Mary who chose to sit at the Lord's feet? (You can find this story in Luke 10:38-42.) She surrendered herself to a beautiful posture. And remember this: My children have only one childhood; we only have these years together once. I only have one lifetime; to hurry and rush through this gift is to completely miss the beauty in it.

Slow. Cherish. Enjoy. Surrender.

Listen

Upon beginning my slow journey, I had an acronym in mind, and my word for L was *less.* I was thinking less clutter, less busying of my schedule, being satisfied with less and how that promotes slow.

As the weeks went by, it really seemed like *listen* might be a better choice, especially when you consider the journey through s.l.o.w.

Listening more naturally follows surrender. Once I have laid my plans in His hands, what I truly need more than anything is to listen to His plan, to read His Word and obey it, to seek His will and follow it, to hear His plan for my day and live it.

We all know that listening involves more than just audibly hearing. It is a taking in and an understanding of what we heard. It is making it our own somehow. How will I internalize what I have heard? How will it change me? How will it impact my day?

It means that I am not the one doing all the talking all the time. I have to close my mouth and employ other senses. I need to know what is best for those around me, not just myself. If you think about it, listening is a form of surrender in and of itself. It is a surrendering of what I want to say right now and an opening of myself to just sit and simply hear and listen.

Listening to God involves being still and quiet, digging into His Word, having a soft heart to receive what we learn, and then a willingness to follow. We'll get into that more in a minute. For now, consider what listening really means. How would listening to God and His Word impact your day for His glory and your good?

Psalm 46:10a, *"Be still, and know that I am God…"*

Proverbs 19:21, *"Many are the plans in a man's heart, but it is the Lord's purpose that prevails."*

Obey

A natural next step after *surrender* and *listen* is *obey*. This was another one that I initially had other ideas about what word to put here. I was thinking *order*. In my human brain, order sounded nice and tidy. It sounded like clearing my schedule of things I did not need/want or that were contributing chaos. But that is how God is, isn't it? He is really much more concerned with our hearts than with our calendars.

Yes, our calendars and the state of affairs in our homes do reflect our hearts and can certainly impact our outlook and attitude. However, the heart of the matter is of considerably more importance. God wants our hearts to be completely His. True slowing can only come with His help, with His guidance, and by obeying His Word.

James 1:22, *"Do not merely listen to the word, and so deceive yourselves. Do what it says."*

Obedience is the overflow of surrendering and listening to God and His Word. It is the outward manifestation of an inward change. As a parent, I endeavor to teach my children to listen and obey as well. God is our heavenly Father and He is the One teaching and instructing us to surrender, listen, and obey.

It is important to note that when we obey, it is not just a drudgery. I talk to my children about obeying all the way, right away, with a happy heart. This is what God wants for our hearts as well— to obey Him all the way, right away and with a happy heart. We have visibly seen the difference in our children and ourselves between begrudgingly obeying and cheerfully obeying. Think of the beautiful testimony that comes from a beautiful obedience to God's Word.

Worship — Is always a battle cry when used ~~let~~ ~~today~~

Overflowing from a heart that is surrendered to God, listening to His Word, and obeying what He has shown us is worship. Worship is thanking God and praising Him for who He is, for His Word, for leading and guiding us, and for His perfect will that is being manifested in us each moment that we are walking according to His Spirit.

Worship is kind of like surrender. We don't always understand the *why* behind what God has asked of us, but we can trust that He is sovereign and does have a perfect plan.

Surrender to Jesus   Correctly
War with the enemy

How can I worship God with the day ahead? With the moments God has given me? If I am rushing through life and trying to see how much I can cram in, where is there room to pause and worship Him? Yet, if I stop and smell a bloom or listen to the snow or sit and let the sun shine down on me and watch the sky for no other reason than to just be quiet, I will see His glory reflected in so many of the everyday, ordinary moments of life.

Moving slow enough to witness His glory will cultivate a hunger to seek more of it and to offer worship and praise back to Him in thanks for the opportunities He sent our way each day. God sends us these gifts every day, but often we are too busy and too frazzled to take the time to pause and enjoy them.

Psalm 100, *"Shout for joy to the Lord, all the earth. Worship the Lord with gladness; come before Him with joyful songs. Know that the Lord is God. It is He who made us, and we are His; we are His people, the sheep of His pasture. Enter His gates with thanksgiving and His courts with praise; give thanks to Him and praise His name. For the Lord is good and His love endures forever; His faithfulness continues through all generations."*

Slow Journal

How does this idea of slow manifested through surrender, listening, obeying, and worship really help you to slow? How does it change you?

> I can worship God
> by understanding
> that even if I don't see
> it he has a plan.
> Even if I don't understand it.

his heart still beats and
chases after me.

S.L.O.W. Word Study

There is no better place to look than God's Word when we want to learn more. I love to take a word that I am learning about and do a word study on it. I will take a concordance and look up every reference in the Bible of that particular word. Frequently, additional words will surface from that one that I can study as well to gain more information and insight into understanding what God wants to instruct to my heart. You will want to pull out your Bible for these next pages!

Let's take each of the four words of our acronym and see what instruction God's Word holds for us. Obviously not every single reference will be included here for the sake of space! I hope if one of these jumps out at you that you will continue to study it further on your own. See Appendix B for more on doing a word study.

Surrender

Before digging into the word study, what comes to your mind when you think of this word: *surrender*? Consider the opposite of surrender and the consequences of a hardened heart toward God.

What do you find freeing about surrendering your day to the Lord and to His plans? What do you find frightening about it?

Now, let's get started! Turn to Jeremiah 37 and read the entire chapter as a way of setting some background. So, there's a new king in town while the reigning king is a captive in Babylon. Describe some of the attitudes you can infer about Zedekiah and his officials from reading verse 2.

In the next verse, the king sends a message to Jeremiah to pray for them. It seems that Zedekiah wants God's favor but isn't interested in any part of surrender, listening, obeying, or worshiping God. God does send Jeremiah a message {vs. 7-10}, which he is able to deliver to the king secretly {vs. 17-18}. However, some of Zedekiah's officials overhear and go to the king, suggesting that Jeremiah does not have the good of the people in mind and should be put to death {38:1-4}.

King Zedekiah has no backbone and simply says, *"It is in your hands, there is nothing I can do to stop you."* {38:5} At this, Jeremiah is thrown into a deep well, where he sinks down in the mud. {38:6} He is rescued by another palace official and brought back before the king. {38:7-14}

Jeremiah faithfully communicates God's words to the king again. {38:17-18}

How does Zedekiah respond to this message? He says, *"I am* _____." {38:19}

Jeremiah provides him a solution to this fear. Look in verse 20 of chapter 38:

- Obey the Lord

- It will go well with you

- You will be spared

He also goes on in the next few verses to explain how the outcome will be different if the king refuses to surrender. {38:21-23}

In the face of struggle, capture, and confusion, Jeremiah is faithfully surrendered to God. We can see a beautiful picture of one who is surrendered and one who refuses to surrender. By looking at the lives of King Zedekiah and Jeremiah, we can see that things end very differently for them.

Look at the verses below and note the outcome for each of these two men. One is a picture of a hardened, un-surrendered heart to Christ, and one is the opposite—beautifully surrendered and serving Christ.

King Zedekiah		Jeremiah	
Verse	*Outcome*	*Verse*	*Outcome*
39:1	Babylon laid siege to Jerusalem	39:11-12	He was looked after, not harmed
39:2	The city wall was broken through	39:14	Returned home, remained with his people
39:4		39:17	
39:5		39:18	
39:6		40:4	
39:7		40:5	
39:8			
52:11			

Consider which side of the chart you would choose to live on today. We may not be in a literal physical war today, but we are most definitely in a spiritual battle. May I propose that Satan loves it when we rush and hurry around because we miss so much of God's purpose in our lives? We gloss over His plans for us and scratch only the surface of living for Him. Use this journaling space to process any thoughts you are mulling over right now.

If you pause to consider, you can probably quickly think of many more biblical characters who were surrendered to Christ. {To name a few: Noah, Daniel, Shadrach, Meshach, Abednego, Mary (Jesus' mother), and even Jesus Christ Himself}. How can their example spur you on toward surrendering to God's plans for you?

Read Matthew 26:36-44. Jesus prays three times for God's will to be done. How can you describe the surrender going on here? What kind of example is Jesus setting for us?

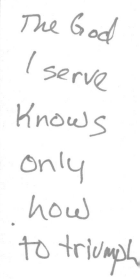

The God
I serve
Knows
only
how
to triumph

When you start your day, consider praying with Jesus, *"Your will be done."* Lay your open hands on your lap as a visual expression of surrender.

From My Slow Journal

Here's a journal entry I wrote down on the edge of a bulletin over a decade ago that illustrates this idea of surrender:

"But when you are invited, take the lowest place, so that when your host comes, he will say to you, 'Friend, move up to a better place.' Then you will be honored in the presence of all your fellow guests. For everyone who exalts himself will be humbled, and he who humbles himself will be exalted." Luke 14:10-11

What I learned today:

I work at a conference center and, today, was scheduled to attend a lunch welcoming our collegiate student summer staff. I would be introduced, get a free lunch, and get to know some of the students. But, God had another plan in mind!

Just as I was preparing to leave my desk - my phone rang and it was a frantic co-worker asking me to please jump in and be the tour guide for the tour which was to have started a few minutes before.

I explained about the meeting, but knew in the back of my mind that the right thing would be to just stay and do the tour. I asked other co-workers, and even felt permission to hand the problem off to someone else. So, I did. And off I went to the meeting.

Before they got ready for our group to be introduced, they discovered the tour was still not taken care of...and they came up with no other option than for me to go back and do the tour.

On my drive back I was crabby, grumbling, complaining and just unpleasant in general. I knew I would be faced with a group of people who were waiting and wondering and maybe even upset. Their tour was to have started almost 30 minutes ago and while they did watch a short video, they still had to wait.

I was also quick to point out to myself that this was one reason I hadn't wanted to be trained to do these tours. And all the way over, I just laid my yucky attitude before God and said, "Lord, I don't want to give this tour and I have a rotten attitude about it."

But, I knew in my heart these people deserved a great tour - the best I could give. I quoted to myself, "Whatever you do - do it all for the glory of God." And, when I was nearly there - the phrase was like a lightning bolt..."Choose the lowest place." A powerful reminder of a passage God had really placed on my heart just a few days ago.

I got to the tour, the people were spectacular and so friendly - we had a delightful time together seeing the beauty of the property. I was indeed blessed by being in their presence. What a God-thing!

But then as I thought more about the passage in Luke - I realized I had few things backwards.

I knew it would be the right thing to go ahead and choose the lowest place and do the tour. In my mind, I set the honorable place on what would bring me glory - being introduced and recognized. But, since I chose the place of "higher" honor - God allowed me to be humbled by having to be *told* to go back and to the tour instead of *choosing* it.

Imagine how much more I would have glorified Him if I had just chosen the lower place <u>first</u>.

Later in the day, thoughts would creep in of wondering if anyone realized what I'd felt like I had sacrificed. If they'd realized I missed lunch and hadn't brought anything because I was planning something different.

But the still small Voice kept saying, "Take the lowest place." And I knew, again, that it was a discipline of the mind that needed to rule over these thoughts.

So, today while many ate pizza, and others saw God's beauty at this beautiful place for the first time - I was on the Potter's Wheel being shaped and re-shaped into the woman God wants me to be! Hallelujah.

Can you think of a time you chose the lowest place or perhaps were forced to choose the lowest place? Describe the situation, how it felt and what you learned.

Listen

Have you ever considered how much God listens to us? He listens to our prayers; He listens to the thoughts of our hearts and minds. He listens to what we say to our children and those around us. He listens, listens, and listens some more.

First, let's take a look at some of the promises of God to be a faithful listener.

Reference	Promise
Psalm 5:1-3	You hear my voice, I wait in expectation
Psalm 10:17	
Psalm 17:6	
Psalm 22:24	
Psalm 34:15	
Psalm 34:17	
Psalm 55:16-17	
Psalm 66:19	
Psalm 86:6-7	
Proverbs 1:33	
Jeremiah 29:12	
Daniel 9:19-23	
John 9:31	

How does it comfort you to see so many examples of God listening to us and to hear His promises for us? Thank God for this right now by writing a prayer to Him.

Now, let's consider the benefits of listening to God and the consequences of not listening to Him. A simple way to understand the consequences is to look at the opposite of the blessings listed.

Reference	Blessing	Reference	Curse/Consequence
Exodus 15:26	Free from diseases, healing	Leviticus 26:14-39	Disease, famine, weakness, etc…
Deut. 5:32-33		Nehemiah 9:17	
Psalm 81:13-14		Psalm 66:18	
Psalm 85:8		Psalm 81:11-12	
Proverbs 1:5		Isaiah 1:15-17	
Proverbs 1:33		Isaiah 30:9	
Proverbs 8:32-34		Isaiah 65:12	
Proverbs 15:31		Jeremiah 6:17-21	
Proverbs 19:20		Jeremiah 7:13-15	
Isaiah 51:1		Jeremiah 11:8	
Isaiah 55:2		Jeremiah 12:17	
Jeremiah 11:4		Jeremiah 13:10-11	
Jeremiah 26:3		Jeremiah 19:15	
		Jeremiah 25:7	
		Jeremiah 44:5-6	
		Ezekiel 8:17-18	
		Zechariah 1:4-6	
		Zechariah 7:12-13	
		Malachi 2:2	
		Acts 3:23	

Luke 8:18, *"Therefore consider carefully how you listen. Whoever has will be given more; whoever does not have, even what he thinks he has will be taken from him."*

I love Isaiah 48:17-19. Let's take a closer look at this passage. It relates blessings of listening and also the opposite – the curses of not listening.

- Read Isaiah 48:17-19

- Verse 17 is dedicated to God's credentials, if you will, a reminder of *why* we should listen to Him. List those reasons here:

He is the Lord

- This prompts me to realize that the only credential I have to my name as to why God "should" listen to me is HIS holiness and salvation. If God did not see Jesus first before seeing me, I would have no right whatsoever to expect Him to listen to me. Even so, I know He will listen to me because He invites me into this fellowship with Him and because His Word teaches and instructs time and again about both the blessings/curses of my listening choices and of His promises to listen when I call to Him.

- Verse 18:

    o *"If only…"* Oh, what a phrase. It is right up there with *What if?* What does the phrase *if only* stir up in your thinking? Think of the tone, the emotions behind it, the truth that backs up who God is, and how our sin hurts our holy and precious God.

    o *"Pay attention!"* I can certainly attest to saying this to my own kids {and really, to my own wandering self, too} and it is usually an unpleasant jolt back to reality. You can remember being in school and having the teacher call you out on something, right? This is God calling us out for "talking in class" or for not paying attention to His commands in this case. Think of a time you were called out on something. How did you respond? Did you get defensive or hold a grudge? Were you repentant and willing to turn things around right away? God is calling on us to listen, to pay attention.

    o And then there is beauty right here for us to witness. The blessings that come to those who *do* listen, who *do* pay attention. List the blessings from the second half

of verse 18 here:

* Peace like …

* Righteousness like the …

o Consider the imagery used. Think of a river. How is it peaceful?

* it' is at times still ~~and~~
* Quiet
* Flowing
*
*
*

o Consider the waves of the sea. List as many ways as you can to describe how this is a blessing when we think of the righteousness we are gifted from God.

* Overwhelming
* Washed in
*
*
*
*

• Verse 19 – continue your list of blessings for listening to God and His commands:

o Descendants like …

o

o

o

• Keep in mind that God is really correcting His people here and saying that these blessings *would have* been theirs *if only.* The opposite of listening is a disregard for God's

Word, His commands. Ignoring. Refusing to hear. Choosing not to listen. Where are you at? Be honest between yourself and God. Are you truly listening to Him? If you need to confess any areas or repent any specifics, take a minute to do that now. Talk to God. *He is listening.*

This is a perfect moment to pause and consider that listening is the first step and obedience is second. Don't worry, we're getting there! There is so much to explore in God's Word, and I love studying it deeply to seek and learn His truth. Let's camp out and listen a little bit longer before we move on.

- Read Isaiah 28:12

- It sounds very much to me like God has provided a place of rest for His people and they won't accept it, won't listen. Put yourself in this verse. Imagine a delightful rest and repose. Describe it here or draw a picture.

Gods given me cornerstone -to Rest 'in' He is my cornerstone

Imagine now that God is holding that out to you and you won't listen to Him to even receive it or be welcomed into that rest. First up, you're crazy! But then again, so am I. You see, we know there is a place of rest in our Lord Jesus. It is the place where we stay close to His heart, we surrender to Him, listen to Him, obey Him, and worship Him. When our souls are at eternal peace with Him, we still need to keep our hearts in a right place in the everyday moments of life. We have things we are afraid of and people we are afraid of.

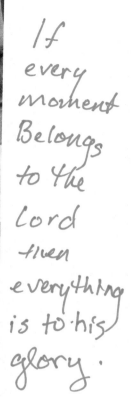

If every moment Belongs to the Lord then everything is to his glory.

- God offers us a place of rest. Will we receive it?

- God offers us eternal peace and place of repose with Him. Have we accepted it? Do we live our lives like we truly accept His free gift of eternal life? {See Appendix A for more on eternal life with Christ!}

  o Reflect on these thoughts here. Jot down things that have jumped out at you, what is resting on your heart, and things you need to take care of or be thankful for. Rest in Him. Find your place of repose in His perfect peace.

Isaiah 50:2, *"When I came, why was there no one? When I called, why was there no one to answer?"*

As we wrap up this section on listening, there is much left unsaid. But let's not depart until we've really considered *how* to listen.

- Consider this: are you spending time in His Word? Are you really *listening* to His voice as you read it? Are you letting it sink deep? Are you having quiet time with Him where you listen to what He lays on your heart? The thing about listening is that there are many options for what we can listen to.

List all the things you listen to during one average day {think people, books, media of all kinds, culture, etc...}

Now, go back and put a star next to the things that help you to listen to God. Put an X next to the ones that detract from you listening to God. Some will be somewhere in the middle; for example, you listen to your kids because God gave them to you. Yes, it probably detracts from how you can listen to God, but they are the calling God has entrusted to you right now, so they are not technically taking away from listening to God. I guess another way to put it would be to consider which things are edifying to your soul and which are not. Which build you up in the ways of God and which do not? If something falls into neither category, you can just skip marking it.

Odds are, you just noticed that you spend a little time listening to God and a LOT of time listening to other things/voices.

I love Isaiah 50:4-5 and how it paints a picture for us of a time to listen and shares more of God's blessings that He promises to us. Write it out here.

What is your morning quiet time like, my friend? I know, I know, life is crazy and little people get up s.u.p.e.r. early. And sometimes they stay up late too, and you are running on empty. That happens at my house too. Here's the thing, it may only be one or two minutes, but it will be SO worth it if we start our day with God. It is a perfect opportunity to slow {surrender, listen, obey, worship} our day before it begins. — I have no excuses — Now is the time to soak up scripture like rain, snow and hurricane

I struggle with these grand plans for my quiet time. I can remember my single days when I could come home from work, put my jammies on, and heat up some leftovers. I could spend the entire evening studying or doing a craft or being quiet. As one who is refreshed by quiet, this was a perfect scenario for me. And sometimes I really want it to exist now, too. Your season right now may look different than mine. You may have too much time on your hands or not enough for various reasons. Our worlds change. God never changes. Hallelujah. The key is SATURATION

I do love to study God's Word, and sometimes I want to spend an hour digging deeper into something I just read. I want to pray, I want to process so many things that my full mind can't always handle during the juggling of children, piano lessons, homeschooling, laundry, dinner,

cleaning ad infinitum. Yet. This is the season God has me in right now. He knows all of those things are awaiting my attention, and He is awaiting my attention too. Not as another thing to do or another box to check off. But as a dearly loved friend who longs for a heart-to-heart chat, to care for my soul, and to invest in me.

What would happen if our tongues were instru[cted]

As a homeschooling mom, I love LOVE the words *instructed tongue*. But truly I love them just as much as a mom or a sister, wife, daughter, or friend. How beautiful to consider the thought of having an instructed tongue. Part of the beauty is in the healing it brings, the beauty it bestows on undernourished souls and downright tired hearts. But a bigger part of the beauty is how we get this instructed tongue: from … the Sovereign Lord. Whoa. *Hosea 14:2*

So if God is instructing my tongue to be used by Him and for His glory, *why don't I listen?!?!?!?!* Ok, I'll stop shouting {at myself}.

Also, we should consider our outside influences and the people we surround ourselves with. What kind of friends would you rather be surrounded by? Friends who are up morning by morning being wakened by the Great Teacher, having their ears opened to learn, being given instructed tongues by the Sovereign Lord? Or friends who don't listen to God and His Word?

It says in verse 4 that this instructed tongue will *"know the word that sustains the weary."* Sometimes that will be me giving a sustaining word to the weary, but let's face it, I will more often than not be the weary one who needs that sustaining word. Sisters, let's be that for each other. Let's listen for the benefits of our precious families and the circles of influence God has seen fit to place us in. Let's also surround ourselves as much as possible with others who listen to Him too so we can lift up and be lifted up through listening to His Word.

When you get up in the morning, you may already have a great quiet time routine. Sometimes we have a great routine for a while but after a longer while goes by we need a reset or jumpstart. If you need a little reboot, start your day surrendering your day to God. Ask for His will for your day. Then just be quiet for a few moments and listen.

What is on your heart? What came to mind? Now your task for the day is to obey anything you heard from God through His Word or even through something He laid on your heart/mind. If you don't know where to read this morning in God's Word, dig into one of the passages we've looked at in these pages. Don't forget to worship. Thank Him for His Word, for caring enough to listen to us, to instruct us, to order our days. Praise Him just because He is God and He is worthy. Oh, He is so worthy.

For further study, consider consulting a concordance and look up passages with the words hear, ear, speak, etc… to learn more about listening to God. See Appendix B for suggestions on how to do a word study.

Obey

Deuteronomy 5:27, *"Go near and listen to all that the Lord our God says. Then tell us whatever the Lord our God tells you. We will listen and obey."*

Obedience should be our natural response to listening. Consider when you give instructions to a child – I don't just talk to hear my own voice! I expect action! We have a saying in our house: *"Obey all the way, right away, with a happy heart!"* Don't you think that kind of obedience from us would delight God's Father heart as well?

James 1:22-25, *"Do not merely listen to the word, and so deceive yourselves. Do what it says. Anyone who listens to the word but does not do what it ways is like a man who looks at his face in a mirror and, after looking at himself, goes away and immediately forgets what he looks like. But the man who looks intently into the perfect law that gives freedom, and continues to do this, not forgetting what he has heard, but doing it – he will be blessed in what he does."*

Let's dig into a little study on this idea. When you hear that word *obey,* does it strike fear into your heart? Does it excite your heart? What perceptions do you have about your level of obedience to God? Take a few minutes and just journal here or speak quietly in your heart before the Lord.

Monica Wilkinson

One of the things with obeying is that there are two sides to it, and they both come with a set of accessories picked out based on how we respond. For example, if we disobey, we should be prepared for consequences and struggle in our lives because of that disobedience. However, there are also beautiful promises given to us in God's Word for those who choose obedience.

Wait, did that just say *choose* obedience? I know. It is often a hard choice, but one that God has given us the freedom to make. Really when we are following our loving God, it is a delight to obey Him and His Word in the deepest part of our hearts. It is not always *easy*, and that is an important distinction to make. Yet, while not always the easiest choice, knowing we choose God's way will always bring us the peace that only He can give.

Let's consider *how* to obey. We'll use the saying from our house mentioned above about obeying all the way, right away, and with a happy heart. I think it is also important to mention that the *happy* heart part may not mean we are super thrilled about what we are being asked to do. I think of it as the posture of our heart. As a sweet friend used to say, "I am not willing, but I am willing to be made willing." Am I willing to be made willing to obey with a happy heart? Is my heart hardened to God or soft? It is also important to remember that obedience does not *earn* us salvation. Obedience is an overflow of the love we have for God. {If would like to know more about receiving Christ as your Savior, please see Appendix A.}

As we are looking, let's notice if there was a blessing or curse attached to their decision. This is far from an exhaustive list, really just a sampling of the mentions of obedience in Scripture. For further study, read Psalm 119 and list all the blessings of obedience and/or consult a concordance and do a word study on obedience vs. disobedience. You could also type in "listen and obey" and look for Scriptures where these occur together. Again, if you would like to know more about doing a word study, see Appendix B.

"And this is love: that we walk in obedience to His commands." 2 John 1:6

Reference	Who?	All the way? Right away? Happy heart? Are one or more of these qualities present?	List any blessing or curse mentioned
Exodus 5:2	Pharaoh	NO!	Destruction of Egypt, plagues
Exodus 19:5-6	Israelites	All the way	God's treasure, holy
Deuteronomy 6:3	Israelites	Carefully obey	Go well, abundant increase and provision
Deuteronomy 6:24-25	Israelites	All the way	Prosperity, life, righteousness
Deuteronomy 11:13-15			
Deuteronomy 11:16-17			
Deuteronomy 15:5-6			
Deuteronomy 21:18-21			
Deuteronomy 26:16-19			
Deuteronomy 30:1-3			
Joshua 1:7-11			
1 Samuel 15:3, 7-9			
2 Chronicles 31:21			
Proverbs 19:16			
Isaiah 1:19-20			
Jeremiah 7:27-29			
Mark 1:17-18			
Luke 2:51-52			
John 14:21			
Romans 6:17-18			
Philippians 2:8-11			

As I was working on the above chart, I was brought back to Deuteronomy over and over again. This book is full of Moses speaking God's words to the Israelites and encouraging them, even challenging and commanding them to obey God. He showed them repeatedly what blessings would come if they obeyed and what curses/consequences would come if they chose to disobey. This encouraged me to dig more into the book of Deuteronomy in my own quiet time, and chapter 11 especially jumped out at me in its relevance to what we are studying here together.

Look at Deuteronomy 11:1-7:

- Obedience is for *you*.

    o Yes, obedience is something we must sometimes require of others in our places of work, at homes, when following the law, and even in our churches. I love how this chapter opens. It is not about pointing the finger at someone else or judging them. No, it is about making sure my heart is in the right place. I am the only one who can take responsibility for my actions. I am the only one who can ensure that I am doing the right things for myself. When God lays something on my heart for obedience, how will I respond? No one else can complete that act of obedience *for me*.

        1. So this begs a question, how do you know when you need to obey God in a certain area? Is it a conviction when you are reading His Word? Is it a nagging feeling that won't leave your mind? Does He wake you up in the middle of the night {like He does me} and strongly remind you to take care of something either right then or first thing in the morning? Take a minute to think about how God communicates to your heart a need for obedience.

        2. Now look at your track record. How do you handle it when He speaks? Do you try to rationalize or justify? Do you promise immediate action and then not follow through? Do you make it your number-one goal for the next day and then *do it*?

        3. Talk to God about these things. Confess or surrender to Him what you struggle with and ask forgiveness for times you do not act in obedience. Ask Him for help, be willing to be made willing, and take the next step He is showing you. Surrender. Listen. Obey. Worship. Slow.

- Obedience is about *remembering.*

  o Another thing I notice in this passage is that there is a focus on God's past faithfulness right after the call to follow God *always.* Why do you think that is? When we remember how God has provided for us, cared for us, proven trustworthy and faithful in the past, we know we can trust Him for the future too. Wouldn't that motivate our obedience? How does remembering motivate obedience for you?

  How has God shown Himself faithful in your life? How can gratitude for His faithfulness fuel your desire to respond in obedience? Consider the Israelites and all that God had just delivered them from. Think about how they would feel in this moment being reminded of God's leading and provisions for them as Moses is asking them to commit to following Him wholeheartedly. Put yourself in their shoes for a moment and jot down anything that comes to mind.

Now, let's continue and read Deuteronomy 11:8-15:

- Obedience gives us *strength* to carry out the plans and purposes God has for us.

  o The Israelites were being delivered from Pharaoh and from wandering in the desert by being offered this new land of blessing. But it wasn't free either. They had a responsibility and a job to do, and that was to follow God and obey Him. There was heavy motivation for following through on this because it offered promise, prosperity, God's blessing, and plenty. Yet consider, the Israelites were humans too. They got tired and hot, and, like we humans are sometimes prone to, they may not have liked change. Maybe they wanted to be content with where they were, maybe they were lazy, maybe they were tired of the next thing or maybe even intimidated and overwhelmed at the idea of the unknown that lay ahead. So Moses jumped right into these thoughts and said in verse 8, *"Observe therefore all the commands I am giving you today, so that you may have the strength to go in and take over the land that you are crossing the Jordan to possess..."*

    1. What is it you need strength for today? This week? This year? Is there a specific way you need to act in obedience to God?

    2. How can obedience give you strength? Try to remember a time when you did follow through on the call to obedience. Recall the peace that came from knowing you took care of it and that you did the right thing. Let yourself be reminded of the strength that comes from God *to* obey and *when* we obey.

   -   Obedience brings *blessing.*

o   Moses spends the next seven verses {Deuteronomy 11:9-15} gushing out the details of the specific blessings that will come from obeying in this particular situation. Take a minute and list them out here:

   1.   Strength _____

   2.   Long life in the promised land

   3.

   4.

   5.

   6.

   7.

   8.

   9.

   10.

o   There are some conditions that were laid out for the Israelites to receive these promises:

   1.   Observe *all* the commands

   2.   Faithfully obey

      Look in verse 13 for two more conditions and list them below.

   3.

   4.

o   So, is blessing to be our main motivation for obeying God? It might be a good kick in the pants, but our main motivation is, of course, our love for God and a response to the way He loves us. Is this a new thought to you? Are these thoughts shaking or confirming your perceptions about obedience? Take a minute to process what is rolling around in your heart and mind.

Read Deuteronomy 11:16-21:

- Obedience is for *singleness of heart.*

    o Just as there are laid out expectations and blessings, there are also cautions. *"Be careful…"* begins this section and is a strong call to stay alert and be aware.

        1. What specifically were the Israelites cautioned to be careful of?

        2. What kinds of things will you need to be careful of? Be specific.

        3 Why? The opposite of blessing is curse, and there are some clear and serious consequences rolled out plainly here. List them {see vs. 17}:

            • The Lord's anger

            •

            •

        4. Can you remember a time that you chose not to obey? What were the consequences? How might things have turned out differently if you had chosen obedience?

        5. Are you single-hearted? Why or why not? Talk to God about the areas of your life and heart that need to be completely obedient to Him.

- Obedience is for *modeling.*

    o This act of obedience is not just for us. We will have people watching us, and if we have woven obedience into the fabric of our lives, it will be a beautiful tapestry for use in God's kingdom.

        1. List all the places we are to *"fix these words"*:

            • Heart

            • Mind

            •

            •

-
-
-
-
-
-

2. Friends, even if there are not little children under your feet, there are children of the faith who need to see the beauty of obedience lived out in you and me. We are the living and breathing children of God, and there should be something different and noticeable, even desirable, about us. How will you model obedience today?

Almost there! Let's read Deuteronomy 11:22-25:

- Obedience is about the *furthering of His name and is for His glory*.

    o Again, the options are beautifully laid out for the people. If you _____ then I will _____. God makes obedience look good! Why oh why do we consistently try to avoid it or try to get our own way? Looking back even just over this one chapter of Scripture we can see over and over the blessings of obedience, the benefits to doing things God's way, and the consequences of choosing otherwise. Yet, we are sinful. We still want what we want just like a two-year-old exerting her own will. Forcefully!

    o As I mentioned above, one of the reasons we obey is to show God to others. These verses confirm this for us in the fact that the way some of these nations are learning about God at all is by watching these foreigners arriving in their land. People will fear God simply because they see the visible expressions of His blessing on His people.

o   I love these four words in verse 22: *"hold fast to Him."* Pause and ponder that thought for a minute. What does that bring to mind?

We went downtown to our local waterfront park the other night for my birthday. A small cruise ship was docking there, and of course our littles were fascinated with all the goings on. The captain was on the top deck calling out instructions, and he had a man a deck below him who was pulling the rope tight. The captain continued to call out the direction to, *"Make it fast"* after each adjustment was made to their position. Make it fast. Hold fast. It is a tight, immovable clinging to safety for us, my friends. Our heavenly captain is on the top deck, and He is calling out to us to *hold fast*. The waters of our culture are choppy and the ride is very rough, but He is in control and He will be glorified. He will empower and strengthen. He will lead and guide and bring us to safety. Rest in that!

Let's finish this chapter off by reading Deuteronomy 11:26-32:

-   Obedience is a *choice*.

    o   It is plainly laid out. What are the two choices offered and what is said about each one?

        1. Blessing:

        2. Curse:

o   I find it interesting and curious that the people were commanded to proclaim their blessings on one mountain and their curses on another. Our deeds will be made known; it is a matter of whether or not they will be made known for God's glory. The choice we make will determine the outcome.

As a result of studying this chapter, what are your thoughts about obedience? Did this change your mind at all or just reinforce what you've already been living out?

I will share my heart with you, friends, that writing this book is an act of obedience. It doesn't matter if it is on Amazon or the NYT bestseller list. It doesn't matter if five people or five hundred people read it. What matters is that I am obedient to what God has laid on my heart. For a long time, I've had the desire to write a book, but I really wanted this to be God's desire, not my own, for His glory alone. I wanted to be confident it was what He wanted.

I started this book and felt His favor and presence but was also doubtful and hesitant. So I set it aside and listened to many of these thoughts that I was not a good enough writer or well known enough to ever get it published or what would others think and what kind of criticism would come from placing myself out there in this form. But God kept bringing me back. A year later, here I am jumping in again in obedience, and He is meeting me here again. Displaying His faithfulness again. He is showing me that the success of this work is not in man's eyes but in the obeying and in the fruit He will bear for His Kingdom.

Another memorable act of obedience led to meeting my husband. I was a single twenty-something working at a place I loved for God's glory. A friend asked if I'd heard of a certain internet matching service for Christians. Immediately, I thought uh-uh, no way. How on earth would I ever tell my future children that their mama and daddy met on the internet? Nope. Not gonna do it.

Then I heard a sermon from John 5 about an invalid who was sitting by the water in hopes that when it was stirred, he would be able to get into the water and be healed. People, he had been

sitting by this pool for THIRTY-EIGHT years. Yes, I am shouting. This is a big deal. Now, an even bigger deal is about to come along. Jesus walks in and uses six words that change his life and have changed mine too. *"Do you want to get well?"*

This man immediately launches into an explanation of how he has no help and everyone else is faster than he is. Jesus senses his real desire, and even though the man never really expressed that he wanted to be healed in direct words, Jesus knows. And Jesus acts. He heals. That is just so Jesus. Here's the thing—after Jesus told this man what to do, the man had to *listen*. He had to *obey*. This is a perfect picture of s.l.o.w. The man was surrendered, he listened, he obeyed, and his living testimony worshipped Jesus.

Even though I was not initially inclined to sign up for an online dating site, God kept bringing this phrase *"Do you want to get well?"* to mind. It was an act of obedience to join the matching service, and six months later I met God's perfect man for me! He had a very similar story about how he was hesitant to join the site, but God used John 5 in his heart and life to bring him to that point of obedience. Through our obedience, God has brought blessing, He has brought glory to His name. So now I ask you: Do *you* want to get well?

Worship

As soon as I got to the end of studying Deuteronomy 11, I noticed the title for chapter 12, *Laws for proper worship*. Here is this natural progression again taking place right in front of our eyes in God's Word to move from surrender, to listen, to obedience, to worship. I'm not going to lay out the laws of worship or even tell you where or how to worship. What I want us to consider instead is why we should worship and what that could look like in a life seeking slow.

When I consider worship in this context, I think of a posture of praise and using my life to worship and serve God. How will this surrendered, listening, obedient heart now worship Him with the time, talents, and treasure I've been entrusted with? How will I enjoy the everyday moments of life He has given? How will I embrace this God-given life and calling? How will I glorify Him today?

My mind instantly went to Matthew 25 and the parable of the talents. You can read verses 14-30 for a refresher, but the Cliff Notes version is that God expects a return on what He has invested in me. Will I offer Him a good Return on Investment? How am I using what He has planted in me?

Secondly, I thought of how I respond to His creation, to His very nature, and how that is worship. When I am truly living out life as myself, I am worshipping Him. Friends, this is another book of its own, because in addition to slow, it is a passion and heartbeat of mine to embrace being the "me" He created for His glory and the blessing of those around me.

Embracing a heart and posture of slow is an act of worship. What is worship? Worship is when I am focusing on Him, bringing Him praise, glorifying Him and thanking Him for who He is. It is also gratefulness for His Word, His faithfulness in my life, and trusting the promise of His continued faithfulness in the future.

When I pull out my camera and notice beauty in creation, this is worship because my heart is in awe of the One who created it and because I am thankful He has allowed me to observe and appreciate it. When I serve dinner to my family with a heart of love, this is worship because I am caring for the needs of others, taking what I have available and nourishing tummies with it, and I am grateful that I have those ingredients to work with. When I stop and enjoy simple moments with my children staring at clouds or listening to the cardinals singing or smelling flowers, this is worship. It is taking what God has given me and enjoying it. In that definition, the rest of this book is about worship. It is about embracing the little moments God has given us and finding beauty in slowing.

As we think about worship, I am reminded of Mary. She sat at God's feet and worshipped, and she was praised for it.

Slow Study: Mary in Three Scenes

Around the time this idea of slow began to form in my heart and mind for the coming year, one of our pastors[1] mentioned Mary {sister of Lazarus} during a sermon. He noted that she was only mentioned three times in the Bible. She is someone who comes to mind when I think of slowing, so I decided to start with the three scenes where we meet and observe her. This is from my own study in each of the three passages.

Scene One: Luke 10:38-42

"As Jesus and his disciples were on their way, he came to a village where a woman named Martha opened her home to him. She had a sister called Mary, who sat at the Lord's feet listening to what he said. But Martha was distracted by all the preparations that had to be made. She came to him and asked, 'Lord, don't you care that my sister has left me to do the work by myself? Tell her to help me!' 'Martha, Martha,' the Lord answered, 'you are worried and upset about many things, but only one thing is needed. Mary has chosen what is better, and it will not be taken away from her.'"

---

[1] Concept shared with permission from Pastor Larry Bennett.

First, look at these differences between Mary and Martha:

- Mary listened; Martha was distracted.

- Mary was focused on Jesus; Martha was focused on herself and her do-list.

- Mary made a slowing choice, a simpler and more peaceful one with long-term benefits; Martha's choices were short-term, busier, and more stressful.

- Mary was quiet, and there are no recorded words or defense; Martha was demanding, frustrated, and sought help.

Now, before it sounds like I'm out to elevate Mary to a pedestal and banish Martha to polishing the floor forever and ever amen, let me note this: Jesus did not say that Martha had chosen *poorly* but that Mary had chosen *better*.

Jesus also said that what Mary chose will not be taken from her. This reminds me of simple yet powerful truths that I need to take time to savor:

- Productivity is fleeting.

- Results do not last.

- Sitting at Jesus' feet has eternal results that will not be taken away.

Perhaps Jesus even wanted us to see that He would not allow Martha's frazzled state to put pressure on Mary and take her from this time with Jesus.

In my life, will I ever regret slowing down? Will I ever regret my hurry? Will I ever regret wishing my house was cleaner? It is interesting that the next thing Jesus teaches about is prayer. Consider that! How do you choose to slow down when you have a God-given personality and gifting that doesn't naturally choose slowing?

Look at that list above and honestly ask yourself which side you would rather live on. For me, it is tricky because there is something to be said for a healthy balance. In daily reality, there is a very real struggle between slowing and productivity. Aside from all the questions, my thought for today is this: How can I make choices that slow? Do the choices I make slow or stress?

Slow Journal

Consider the questions mentioned in Scene One of Mary's study. Go into as much or as little detail as is helpful for you.

In your life, will you ever regret slowing down?

Will you ever regret hurry?

Will you regret wishing your house were cleaner?

Looking at the compare/contrast between Mary and Martha, which side do you fall on right now? Which side would you rather live on? Why?

How can you make choices that slow? Do the choices you make slow or stress?

Scene Two: John 11

While it is too long to share this entire chapter here, take a few minutes to read through it. Here are a few thoughts that came to mind after reading this passage.

First of all, I notice in verse 6 that Jesus was not in a hurry but on God's timetable. Think of how you would have responded to this need. How would your own hurry have added unnecessary stress?

Slow is showing patience. I see how Martha heard that Jesus was coming and she ran out to meet Him {busy, anxious, excited} and Mary stayed home {quiet, slow, peaceful, patient}. See verses 17-20.

When Jesus arrived, Martha began her chattering right away {likely due to grief and nerves} and Jesus turned it into a teachable opportunity. Jesus stayed outside the village where He met Martha and was asking for Mary, so Martha went to get her. Mary responds to Jesus' call quickly. She is an example of calm but is ready to act when her Lord calls upon her. I love this!

Mary is at Jesus' feet again weeping, and her only recorded words are mentioned here. Both Mary and Martha show their faith by their words that if Jesus had been there, Lazarus would have lived. Mary places herself in a humble position before Jesus.

Hurry is a desperate grasping to maintain control while slow is a submitted willingness to choose peace. Hurry strives for perfection and control. Slow humbly embraces surrender.

Consider this: How do you feel around one in a hurry versus someone who is choosing slow?

Scene Three: John 12:1-11

After you've had a few minutes to read these verses, here are a few things related to slow that I observed:

- Martha was serving. They slowed to open their home in hospitality.

- Mary's heart is about worship. Maybe slowing is a state of the heart and mind more than anything?

- Mary was a beauty-seeker: peaceful, calm, and slowing allow embracing and creating of beauty, choosing Jesus, and worship.

- Mary was extravagant; it was an expensive gift!

- Mary was not worried with what others thought even though she was criticized.

- Mary's gift brought beauty to all through the scent that permeated the house.

- Jesus defends Mary. Again.

- I found this note written in my Bible, *"Worship gives up convenience."*

- For context and connecting when events took place, the next day was the entry on a donkey with palm branches.

Slow Journal

What do you think about the possibility that slowing is a state of the heart and mind more than anything?

Process this thought, *"Worship gives up convenience."*

How can you mentally, physically, and spiritually slow down?

Understanding Slow: Your Turn

After spending quite a bit of time considering this posture of a SLOW heart, how has this trickled into your heart and mind? What is God putting on your heart? Spend some time processing what you've studied and taken in so far. Write out a prayer to God, go for a walk and talk to Him, or sit and make a list of things you were reminded of or learned.

A Slow Heart Retreat

Every summer, I try to take one day or big chunk of a day for a heart retreat. This is a time where I go somewhere quiet by myself to sit with God and really seek Him for our upcoming school year. What is He saying to me? What needs to change? What are our problem areas that I need guidance/ wisdom on? What can I learn about any of these from His Word?

I love taking a personal retreat so much that I want to help you envision how to make it a reality in your own life. If this sounds appealing to you, read on!

Like me, you may have to make arrangements in order to plan something like this. Who will care for your children? What will they eat? Where will you go? What will you eat? I hope by sharing a few things that have worked for me, it will encourage you to consider how to make this a reality in your schedule.

Why a Quiet Heart Retreat?

* Being *still*. Frequently, I probably spend the first hour doing nothing but just being still. Not doing anything, just sitting. My favorite place to have my retreats is outside enjoying God's creation and listening to small sounds that are usually too overcrowded with noise to hear or notice. Psalm 46:10, *"Be still and know that I am God."*

* We are *invited*. By example, Jesus invites us to get away alone and spend alone time with our heavenly Father. No, this isn't saved for a once-a-year-retreat! But, it is the perfect model for us of leaving the noise and moving ourselves to a solitary place to be with Him. Mark 1:35, *"Very early in the morning, while it was still dark, Jesus got up, left the house and went off to a solitary place, where he prayed."*

* It is *refreshing*. I know we aren't all wired the same, but time to sit quietly and be rejuvenated is something of great benefit even if we are only able to make it happen once in a while. Our lives are so noisy and busy. Time to just think is precious and rare. Quiet and stillness are refreshing and life giving. The Sabbath itself was established for rest *and* refreshment. Exodus 31:17, *"It will be a sign between me and the Israelites forever, for in six days the Lord made the heavens and the earth, and on the seventh day he rested and was refreshed."*

* It is a great way to *refocus*. I can get tunnel vision sometimes. I'm too close to a situation or too immersed in it, and stepping back and widening my view can be very helpful and provide some great perspective. Summer has been a great time for me to have these retreat days because with a new school year starting, it is a good time to evaluate many things. 2 Corinthians 5:7, *"For we live by faith, not by sight."*

Planning Your Retreat

As you begin to pursue this idea of planning your Quiet Retreat, here are some things to consider:

* Make it a *priority*. If it is important to you to make it happen, you will make it a priority! Schedule a day, put it on your calendar, and look forward to it! Jot down ideas or thoughts that continue to surface in your mind and heart and plan to spend time pursuing those thoughts more and seeking God's Word for insight into these areas.

* *Plan* for your family. Obviously this will only be a success if you have adequate care for your family! My personal opinion is that this retreat is such a blessing to my own heart that it is a blessing to my family as well. Arrange childcare, make plans for what they will eat while you are away, think

ahead for dinner when you get home. Spending your time away worrying about what your family is doing or what you will serve for dinner when you return will not be of any benefit! Do all that you can to see to these things ahead of time.

* Plan for *your* retreat. Not only do you need to have your family cared for, but I have found it helpful to do some planning for my retreat as well. As I mentioned above, I jot down words or thoughts that are consistent in my thinking near the time of the retreat. Or, if I have any specific things I am wanting to process, pray about, or implement in our home, I might write these thoughts down as well. Before I go, I usually take one, two, or three words or thoughts and look them up in the Bible or a concordance. I will write down the reference to passages that mention that word or idea. I don't look them up yet, but I just make a quick list of places to start when I get to my retreat. Sometimes one of those thoughts emerges higher than the others, or sometimes a whole new passage comes to light, but it is a place to start. You can learn more about doing a word study in Appendix B. If I don't have some idea of where to start, I think it puts pressure on me to have a spiritually invigorating day which can be difficult when I have not invested any forethought. It is not a recipe for success. Think ahead about what you will eat. Do you need to bring lunch or can you find a nice lunch spot to enjoy? If you are planning to be outside, is there a back-up for bad weather?

* Be *flexible.* I tend to over plan. I have my list of passages I want to look up and thoughts I want to study. I also bring a journal, my Bible, of course, and even one or two books to just read. This way, I can go with what works for me that day and be flexible with myself.

Two years in a row, it rained in the afternoon on my retreat day. One time I found a spot inside, and another year I sat under a covered bench. If I decide I want to go for a walk, I do! I allow myself to not have to be rigid about a specific schedule but to go with what feels refreshing.

I readily admit that my retreat days are spent in ideal circumstances. My parents watch my children, my mom plans dinner, I frequently have lunch out with a friend, and I have an amazing place to go. It is such a priority and habit to me now, though, that I would be willing to pay a babysitter if needed to keep this going.

I hope you will be encouraged to consider the idea of how to make this a reality where you are as well. Find a park or garden where you feel at peace and will be undisturbed. Ask God to help you if this is a desire in your heart.

- Where can you go?

    o   A park or other quiet/calming outside place

- o   Church prayer room or a spare room someone is not using

- o   Coffee shop if you can study with a little bit of noise

- o   Study room at the library

- o   Your car—parked in a quiet park or safe scenic overlook

- o   A hotel room if you are able to get away for an overnight

- o   Your own house if you can make arrangements for those who share that space with you and won't be distracted by to-do's around you!

- o   Bookstore reading area, restaurant in a quiet corner, or at a friend's house who is out for the day.

- o   The point here is that you can get creative, even if you have to lock your bedroom door and put a sign on it that you are not available. Consider what could work best for you.

- How long should it be?

   This is entirely dependent upon what you can work out, what works best for you, and if this is something new to you or not. If you've taken personal retreats before or have a particularly stressful set of circumstances, you may need a longer time! I have varied between 3-8 hours on my Quiet Retreats, but I would try not to go less than 2 or 3 hours. It can take quite a bit of time at the beginning just to quiet your heart and focus on listening since you are stepping out of ordinary life and trying to really slow and pause.

- What should you bring?

- o   Bible

- o   Journal

- o   Water and/or food/snacks if you will be gone over a meal time. Plan this in advance so you won't spend valuable retreat time figuring out a simple detail like hunger and thirst!

- o   Pens or preferred writing utensils

- o   Camera

- o   Two or three topics that are on your heart, if applicable, that you could process through.

o   A craft – one year I brought watercolor paints on my Quiet Retreat and enjoyed a time of just creating in a peaceful place. It was very refreshing and therapeutic, but it is not something I've done every time. Again, consider your own special personality and see what would be a good fit for you.

o   A sweater – temperatures inside and out can fluctuate over a few-hour time period. Be prepared to stay comfortable and not allow something like that to distract you from the special set aside time.

o   Anything else you can think of that would be a blessing to you during your time. I like quiet, but if you like music, bring ear buds and whatever you listen to music on.

How do you get started?

If you've gotten through all of the logistics and planning and are now on your Quiet Retreat, you may have just plopped down and thought, *"Now what?"*

I've written this section to walk you through having your own retreat. You will find suggestions and examples from one of my retreats. You may want to bring this book with you on your retreat for some ideas or look through it ahead of time and jot a few thoughts down to take with you.

Each of my Quiet Retreats have looked just a little bit different. The one I'm going to share now was specifically focused on this idea of slow and the words surrender, listen, obey, worship. This is just an idea or a starting place; there is no magic formula, and I hope you will be open to what comes and seems to be right at the time. Let God lead!

I usually begin my retreat by sitting quietly sometimes even for a whole hour. It takes some time of quiet and doing almost nothing to transition from the input of life to a quiet peace. Consider this first segment of time - *slowing to listen*. On one retreat, I wrote out Psalm 46:10, *"Be still and know that I am God."* And then I just sat quietly. I wrote down the sounds I heard like the breeze through the aspen leaves, birds chirping at a fountain, silverware clinking, and more. This is a chorus of praise - creation praising Him, people serving, time slowing, breeze blowing, water trickling.

You can make a short list if you want to of the sounds you hear. Or you can sit in stillness and quiet and write a list of thoughts swirling around in your head and heart. What is God laying on your heart? What are your purposes for this time of reflection? What do you want to hear from God about?

Don't be in a hurry to move past this part. Just sit, slow, savor, listen, be quiet.

I can't tell you how many times in the past year or two I've made myself take a deep breath and just think over these words to myself:

surrender . . . listen . . . obey . . . worship . . .

Surrender. Matthew 11:28, *"Come to me, all you who are weary and burdened, and I will give you rest."*

Think for a moment. What does surrender mean to you? Write down thoughts that come to mind. What things do you need to surrender? Write down everything you can think of.

I was journaling on a scrapbook paper at the time and loved the little bubble design on the page. It struck me that the bubbles float up and away from me and that is such a picture of surrender and letting go.

Spend as much or as little time as suits you on this pondering of surrender. Consider what it means and what it means to you, your heart, your life, and serving God.

Listen.

When you are ready to move on {or even another day}, begin thinking about the idea of *listening*. What does that mean to you? What does that look like in your life?

What kinds of things do you spend time listening to? What influence do the things you listen to have on your life?

Do any of these influences need to go or need to be cultivated because they are beneficial?

How are you listening to Jesus? How are you listening to His Word?

Continuing in Matthew 11, think about verse 29, "*Take my yoke upon you and learn from me, for I am gentle and humble in heart, and you will find rest for your souls.*" I hope you are feeling slow seep into your heart, mind, and spirit as you process through this. There is no right or wrong way!

Obey.

Continuing on in your retreat, or again it can be another day, look at the word *obey*. Ponder Matthew 11:30, *"For my yoke is easy and my burden is light."*

What words, thoughts, or phrases come to mind when you think of obeying? Spend your desired amount of time processing obedience for yourself.

What in your life right now needs your obedience? Something that came to my mind is the thought that first-time obedience is not just for children. Ponder that one for a few minutes.

Is God asking you to obey Him in something right now? What decision can you make to begin acting on that and following Him in it? Pray and talk to God about this.

Worship.

Now we move to *worship*. You can write out any verses that come to mind, sing a praise song, pray and thank God, write down things you are thankful for, etc... This is not a recipe for what to do; it is just one idea. Quietly reflect in your heart with an attitude of worship being thankful and praising God for the time you have spent with Him.

By this point, you may have spent about three hours reflecting, journaling, thinking, and praying. Does it sound ridiculous to say that it takes several hours to get through the beginnings of a retreat like this? I have done this annually, and it is different every time, but the one constant is that I need time at the beginning {usually about an hour} just to sit and breathe and listen and do nothing. The point is this: just be still and let it come. Don't try to force your time; that sort of defeats the purpose! After walking through my slow thoughts, we are ready to process the blessings of slow. Write a letter to God or jot down thoughts/phrases or whatever comes to mind about the blessings of slowing or another topic dear to your heart.

Sometimes when pursuing a lifestyle like this, it is helpful to consider all the blessings and benefits of staying the course. And it is another great opportunity for praising and worshiping God as we realize all the blessings that come from following through.

After finishing this, I moved on to another word that has been on my mind. *Enough.* Did you see the <u>*Mom's Night Out*</u> movie? I really liked it, and my favorite part was when one of the moms was sitting and talking to a biker dude and pouring out her heart about how she is not enough. This rough and tough guy says back to her, *"Enough for WHO?"*

That has really stuck with me because I frequently feel like not enough, but no one in my family is saying I'm not enough and God is not saying I'm not enough. I am saying I am not enough for me. In light of all that, I had wanted to spend some time processing that idea of enough.

I did a little journaling and then went for a walk and took photos, which is energizing and fun for me. That's it.

It was not earth shattering yet very refreshing. It was peaceful, relaxing, intentional, quiet, reflective and slow. It was not perfect, but it was just right.

Slow Journal

What are your thoughts about having a retreat day?

What appeals to you about a retreat?

What scares you about a retreat?

Brainstorm some places you could possibly go for a quiet retreat.

How do you think this may be beneficial for you and your family?

PART THREE
A Slow Life

No Rush: How can I slow when there is so much to do?

There's no rush! Has anyone ever said those words to you? You can instantly feel a difference between the stress of hurry and the peace of take your time. My husband, David, started saying this to me years ago, and it has taken me a while to embrace it. No rush. That brings such freedom, such peace. I have observed over and over how much I hate feeling rushed. It adds pressure, stress, and a heaviness and edge to my voice and demeanor. It is so much easier to be kind and loving when I am not in a rush.

But let's be honest, sometimes we are in a rush, as I admitted earlier. Pretty soon we realize it is time to go, we're five minutes late, one child can't find his shoes, and the phone is ringing, and there it all goes: downhill. Again.

There is no easy one-size-fits-all recipe for fixing this, but I think there are some ingredients that have consistently helped me. Maybe you can see this as a build-your-own buffet of ideas to pick what might work for you or to spur you on toward something similar you already do or even come up with your own idea!

Starting the Day with God

You've heard this one before. It's not a newsflash or new idea! Yet it is worth repeating and I'm preaching to myself again. Starting the day with my Bible takes discipline; it's another choice between obedience and disobedience, another opportunity to surrender and listen and worship.

In fact, sometimes I will approach my time with God by walking through this acronym of s.l.o.w. I surrender this day to You, Lord. I will listen to Your Word and obey it. Help me to spend this day worshiping You in light of what You showed me this morning.

What if you aren't sure where to start? Honestly, sometimes this is why I don't start my day with God. I've finished what I was working on before and am not sure what to move on to next. I'm looking for something life-changing, and a lot of times it is not earth shattering enough. However, I think the key is just *to start*, to read *something*, to be with God in some way at the beginning of your day.

Here are some ideas to get you going:

- Read Proverbs. With 31 chapters, you can easily read one a day each month. Match the date to the chapter and there you go. Proverbs is loaded with great wisdom for daily life, and I frequently find myself taking a thought with me through the day after reading Proverbs.

- Do a word study. This is my very favorite way to study God's Word. I pick a word that I want to know more about or that is on my heart, and then I dig in and see what I can learn. You can learn more about how to do a word study in Appendix B.

- Pick a book of the Bible. I also love to do this; I will start at the beginning of one book {such as Deuteronomy, which I've been reading through lately} and just read one or two chapters a day. It is a great opportunity to visit some of the lesser-known books and get a new perspective on what is being laid out in that book. I love the Old Testament books for this!

- Read the Psalms. With an abundance of chapters, Psalms seems to always be encouraging and real. David, one of several authors of the Psalms, pours his guts out in many of these chapters, and I think we can relate to that. If you are feeling down, discouraged, or overwhelmed by enemies, you will likely find some strength, courage, or comfort by reading a psalm.

- There are lots of Bible studies and books and resources you can reach for, but my personal preference is to keep this morning time for just God, His Word, and you. I can do Bible studies at other times if that is what will be of benefit, but I don't like to crowd out God's voice with other voices during this time.

After I've had some time with Him, I will sometimes grab a piece of paper and think about what I need to get done that day. I've been known to write out the acronym for *slow* again and consider what parts of my day will be spent in surrender, listening, obedience, and worship. Where surrender and listen are quiet and on the receiving end, obedience and worship are on the action end of

things. How can I implement what I learned in my time with God? How can I please Him in how I spend my time in the day set before me? How can I choose a heart posture of slow? How can I physically slow today?

Under Commit and Remember Balance

Over-committed. We've heard of that, right? Many of us are over-committed right now, have been in the past, or will be in the future. It seems to be the way of the world these days. But would you pause with me and consider God's example?

I am typically efficient with my time and a very productive worker. *But* I have found that the more efficiently I work, the more I want to get done and the harder it is for me to slow down. Can anyone relate?

It's like a frenzy that feeds itself and generates a vicious cycle. It goes something like this: I may be feeling overwhelmed and want to get more organized and on a better routine. I will plan out my day and get up early and get going. Crossing things off my list feels great, and I have a productive day, hoping days like this will never end. I think of how much I can get done if I can maintain this level of speed and efficiency, but let's face it, I do not allow room for slowing on my "list."

I may have a few good days like that, and then pretty soon I'm getting tired sooner than I used to. I'm starting to get discouraged and get less done, and it isn't long before half of my list may still be staring at me before the end of the day. After that, I give up on the list and just start letting the days flow the way they will. This is more relaxing, but I find that I get less done and begin to feel overwhelmed, and so the cycle has come full circle and starts all over again.

On the other side, I've found that if I slow down too much it feeds this desire to slow down *too* much. You know how that works, right? My kids are playing great, and I'm on the couch reading a book, for example. I realize we should get on to the next chore or piece of business to keep our day flowing smoothly. This is a tricky spot to be caught, because on one hand I will think there is no way I'm messing with it while they are happily engaged playing with one another, so I might just read some more of my book.

Frequently when I do that, though, I find that those extra minutes can be when the sweet spot we were in goes sour. An argument will break out among the young ranks of my home, or they will just get tired of getting along. If I had intervened *before* things got to this point, it would've served me well. But slowing was calling also.

This is proof positive that slow is a balance. We can neither ignore slow completely nor give in to it completely. Like so much of life, isn't it?

Here is a real list I wrote for myself {and I am not encouraging this!} one day, and I did get every single thing done. But to what end? I was probably a drill sergeant marching out orders to all of my little soldiers, and I can pretty well guarantee that I did not spend much quality time with them.

So, how can we reconcile productivity with slowing? This is a question I have savored and thought about a lot and will probably continue to process and wrestle with.

As I pondered that, God brought it to mind to go back to Genesis and read the Creation account. If you want to read it right now, go to Genesis 1:1-2:3.

Let's face it: as women, wives, mothers, sisters, daughters, friends, and more, we have a lot to do. We also have a lot more we *could* do, and we must learn to prioritize and balance what we *need* to get done and what we *want* to get done. I'm so thankful that we have God's Word and a beautiful example before us in God Himself and in His Son Jesus for how we can balance slow and productivity. Today, I'm looking at God the Father through the lens of Creation. Lessons learned from God:

* He took time to enjoy and appreciate what He accomplished each day. At the end of every day, He paused and reminded us what He had created that day and said it was good. I don't know about you, but I am notorious for moving on to the next thing{s} without appreciating the satisfaction of completing the thing{s} before. This is the downside of always working ahead: I'm always thinking to what I need to do next so that as soon as I finish one thing, I know what to move on to.

* He was under-committed each day; He worked under His potential. God modeled for us how to choose one or two things to focus on each day. The thing is that if He wanted to, He could have spoken the entire world into existence in less than a fraction of the blink of an eye. But He did not. He went about it methodically, slowly, with balance and moderation. Oh, what I could learn from that. I've talked recently about being under-committed. God was not looking to maximize every

productive waking moment of every single day. He chose to focus on one or two things, do them well and with excellence, and then enjoy the accomplishment and reflection of a job well done.

* He modeled rest. Not only did He NOT fill each day with a mile-long list of tasks to finish and no time to take a breath, He is the author of the very first Slow Day: the Sabbath. We observe the Sabbath in our home but also an additional Slow Day {we'll get to this more in depth in a few pages} where we definitely do work but also strive to bring the pace down, expect less in terms of productivity, and worship God throughout. I think He also modeled rest by not filling every day to maximum capacity and by creating evening and morning—different times of day for different needs.

* He did not model multitasking. As already mentioned above {but worth mentioning again!}, God did not model how to cram tasks together nor did He emphasize huge amounts of productivity but instead chose one or two things to focus on each day. How would this transform my life if I focused on a few quality things: my walk with God, schooling my children, family, and a moderate amount of maintaining our home?

* Finish. God modeled for us how to stick with that one thing until it is finished rather than flit from thing to thing never really finishing anything. I know you've all been there—you get up to go put your glass away in the kitchen. On the way, you see a sock that needs to go in the dirty clothes, so you deliver that. While in that area, you see a shelf that needs organizing or towels that are not folded neatly, so you stop and take care of that. Next, the phone rings, a child asks for something, or someone comes to the door, or even all of those things at once, and you are still carrying your glass around who knows how long later. Are you smiling out of identifying with that? One time when my mom was at our house, we were talking about how hard it is to get things done in the season of life with young children. She observed that I had trouble finishing one thing and had multiple things going at once. I have really tried to take this to heart and finish one thing before starting another; it is hard to do but worth the effort of attempting to make it more and more of a habit.

* God worked with an end goal in mind and worked toward that in daily-sized chunks. I love also that He had a beautiful end result in mind when He began His work of creating the world. He knew there would be trees, flowers, animals, people, seasons, planets, and more. Then He methodically worked through the days in a chosen order until the desired results were accomplished. This is a good reminder for me to consider what my end goals are and how my daily investments of time and energy are contributing.

To sum it up, God sets a beautiful example of not cramming every day to the fullest. He shows us how to balance productivity and slow, how to enjoy the feeling of accomplishment, and how to leave room for His opportunities that arise each day. He models being under-committed and savoring the gift of rest.

What one thing will you take from God's example and begin to prayerfully implement into your slowing?

Figure out a Routine

Are you a routine person? I definitely am! But I think I would describe it more like flexible outline rather than rigid routine. Guidelines, boundaries, knowing what to expect and how to plan/prepare—all of those things are calming to me. So I ask you this: how can having a routine, of whatever sort works for you, help you slow?

Sometimes slow will just happen, and sometimes you will have to make it happen. When you have a flexible guideline of the ideal way your family likes to spend their time, it may help in the spontaneity of slowing.

For example, if I'm standing in front of my fridge with the door open and just staring inside at 5:00 p.m. wondering what on earth is for dinner tonight, I'm going to struggle to slow at the table and be willing to really talk to those seated with me. What are those things you will encounter in everyday life that you can plan on doing and be prepared for so that you can embrace slow when the opportunity presents itself?

We will always need to eat, and we will always need to keep the house somewhat in order. Take a minute and consider if there are things that are consistently putting you in a situation of stress or hurry. Now pause and pray. Is there something you could do differently to alleviate some of that? How could you choose slow in even one thing this week?

Here's my scenario. When I'm disciplined and really motivated, I have good systems in place to manage everyday things. Yet so often I find myself getting tired and worn down from asking

again that I start to give up, which starts a downward spiral toward being overwhelmed. Once I arrive at overwhelmed, it is really hard to pick myself up and get going again because, ahem, it is so *overwhelming.*

I like to write out my "ideal" framework of a schedule. Not because every day is even remotely close to ideal, but because it gives me a goal to work toward. And above all of that to remember that it is my goal to please God. {2 Corinthians 5:9}

This brought to mind a life purpose that I wrote out years ago from Colossians 1:10-14. {I have inserted personal pronouns for more personal impact.}

"It is my goal and desire to live a life worthy of the Lord and that I might please Him in every way; bearing fruit in every good work, growing in the knowledge of God, being strengthened with all power according to His glorious might so that I may have great endurance and patience, and joyfully giving thanks to the Father, who has qualified me to share in the inheritance of the saints in the kingdom of light. For He has rescued me from the dominion of darkness and brought me into the kingdom of the Son He loves, in whom I have redemption, the forgiveness of sins."

I personally please God more in my attitude and demeanor when things are running smoothly in my home regularly. Of course, things happen; hiccups interrupt service, so to speak. But making it my regular habit is such a blessing to myself and therefore those whom I am privileged to serve.

Some specific things that help me are:

- FlyLady: {www.flylady.net} If you need someone to hold your hand {like I do} in knowing what to do and when and who will remind you to do it, this website is for you! You may also enjoy the book *Sink Reflections* by Martha Cilley, founder of the FlyLady website. I love her suggestions of having certain chores assigned to certain days and try to do the daily missions whenever possible to keep up on those lesser-known chores. You can look at the website for the daily missions or subscribe to a weekly email which lists the entire week ahead. I am also so encouraged by the fact that she says, "Whatever we *can* get done still blesses our homes." It's not about focusing on what we can't get done but on the blessing of what we were able to accomplish that day.

- Home Blessing Hour: This is another favorite of mine and also an idea from FlyLady. Her suggestion is to pick six things {vacuum, bathrooms, dust} and once a week spend ten minutes on each one. In one hour, you will have accomplished a lot and feel great about your home with a small investment of time. My mom is my accountability partner in this!

- Freezer cooking: I've done many variations of freezer cooking, but this continues to be something that blesses my family and allows my time to be more flexible and efficient. Whether you make a freezer full of food all at once or cook double and freeze half or even just keep chopped, cooked chicken in your freezer, you may find that it is a blessing to you at dinnertime when you have some quick options available. If another system is better for you, by all means go for it!

- Staying home: When we spend lots of time out of our house, it shows. For us, I've learned that being home more than we are gone is one way we can maintain order, get our chores done, and choose slow more often!

Psalm 16:6, *"The boundary lines have fallen for me in pleasant places; surely I have a delightful inheritance."*

How does that prove true for you? What boundaries do you have in place that bring delight and pleasantness?

When sharing at church one Fall with a group of homeschool moms, we talked about how our work will be undone before our eyes. We need to figure out what we are fixing for dinner and, oh no, the kids are arguing again, the phone is ringing, and the house is a disaster. Please tell me this is not just me? Friends, we are in this together, and if you are like me, I fail a lot. I want to accomplish more, be happier and more positive to my children, lose it less, and need grace to try again tomorrow. Are you with me?

We're not going to talk specific schedules or anything, because we all have enough expectations, comparing, judging, and Pinteresting going on to last us forever. We need Jesus. We need His Word.

So first I have to ask, what is your goal? That is always helpful in knowing why you are doing what you are doing and how to go about it. In the midst of messy, busy, ordinary life, I want to be like wisdom. She is described so beautifully in Proverbs 3. Read the whole chapter when you can, but for right now, let's look at verses 17-18:

"Her ways are pleasant ways and all her paths are peace. She is a tree of life to those who take hold of her; those who hold her fast will be blessed."

Take a deep breath and let that sink deep. I heard such beautiful, descriptive words:

- Pleasant

- Peaceful

- Brings life

- A blessing

Dear ones, isn't that what we so desperately want? To please God by seeking His wisdom and to be described as beautifully as she is? I want to be a vessel of peace, pleasantness, blessing, and life. Notice I said a *vessel* and not the *source*. There is a big difference. A vessel is formed by another and used by another. Yes. So that is my goal.

While listening to a webinar, a seasoned home school mom shared that she and her children had read Genesis 1 together, and her children noticed that the phrase *evening and morning* was repeated six times. She figured that if these times of day were so important to God, perhaps she should spend some time focusing on those times in her home as well.[2] This got me to thinking too. What else did God's Word say about evening and morning? I have to admit these are two areas my family struggles with. We are not as consistent with bed time, rise time, and routines as I wish we were, and sometimes it is downright chaotic. So I went hunting for treasure in God's Word. Perhaps one or both of these times of day are a challenge for your family as well.

God said there was evening and morning; time was measured differently in those days. Sundown to sundown was a day. Since God said evening first, let's start there. It strikes me that our evening patterns and decisions can affect our next morning as well! These are very influential times of our day. Have you noticed? If I get up later than I hoped, it throws my morning out of whack, which may indeed throw my whole day. If I do not get my children or myself into bed at a good time, it steals peace and restfulness, and then I have trouble waking up in the morning. And even as we talk about evening and morning, I think you will have to define what those exact times mean in your home. For me, morning is before breakfast and evening is after dinner. That is how I am

---

[2] The webinar was presented by Jennifer Courtney and based on an article titled, *"Morning and Evening: Setting a Rhythm for the Day."* Article and webinar are copyrighted material of Classical Conversations MultiMedia, Inc.

framing my thoughts in my mind, but again that is going to take many different shapes in many different homes.

Let's take a look at what the Bible has to say about evening.

Genesis 24:62-63, *"Now Isaac had come from Beer Lahai Roi; for he was living in the Negev. He went out to the field one evening to meditate, and as he looked up, he saw camels approaching."*

Picture the scene: a field is quiet and solitary, evening light is different, and it has a quieting affect to our heart. A field is a beautiful picture of a place that brings life and nourishment. Evening is for quieting our hearts and focusing on God and His Word—a feeding of our souls.

Exodus 16:11-13, *"The Lord said to Moses, 'I have heard the grumbling of the Israelites. Tell them, "At twilight you will eat meat, and in the morning you will be filled with bread. Then you will know that I am the Lord your God."' That evening quail came and covered the camp, and in the morning there was a layer of dew around the camp."*

God provided food for the people twice a day; we saw soul food in the first passage, and now we see physical food. Evening is for nourishment.

Ruth 2:17-18, *"So Ruth gleaned in the field until evening. Then she threshed the barley she had gathered, and it amounted to about an ephah. She carried it back to town, and her mother-in-law saw how much she had gathered. Ruth also brought out and gave her what she had left over after she had eaten enough."*

Evening is for a ceasing of work and nourishment from food.

Psalm 104:23, *"Then people go out to their work, to their labor until evening."*

Evening is for a daily end to work. Consider this as moms when we don't leave our workplace and the work is never done. Do we stop work?

Zechariah 14:7, *"It will be a unique day – a day known only to the Lord – with no distinction between day and night. When evening comes, there will be light."*

Morning and evening are earthly boundaries of time. God is not limited by these boundaries, but He is the Creator of them.

Matthew 26:20-30, *"When evening came, Jesus was reclining at the table with the Twelve. And while they were eating, He said, 'Truly I tell you, one of you will betray Me.' They were very sad and began to say to Him one after the other, 'Surely You don't mean me, Lord?' Jesus replied, 'The one who has dipped his hand into the bowl with me will betray Me. The Son of Man will go just as it is written about Him. But woe to that man who betrays the Son of Man! It would be better for him if he had not been born.' Then Judas, the one who would betray him, said, 'Surely you don't mean me, Rabbi?' Jesus answered, 'You have said so.' While they were eating, Jesus took bread, and when He had given thanks, He broke it and gave it to His disciples, saying, 'Take and eat; this is My body.' Then He took a cup, and when He had given thanks, He gave it to them, saying, 'Drink from it, all of you. This is My blood of the covenant, which is poured out for many for the forgiveness of sins. I tell you, I will not drink from this fruit of the vine from now on until that day when I drink it new with you in my Father's kingdom.' When they had sung a hymn, they went out to the Mount of Olives."*

This is probably my favorite picture of an evening – reclining, eating together, conversation, singing a hymn, going for a walk. We can do beautiful slowing with our dear families. How many times do you jump up from the dinner table to clean up, change the laundry, and get back to work? Again, here is the picture that we need to aim for in a finishing of work for the evening.

Acts 4:3, *"They seized Peter and John and, because it was evening, they put them in jail until the next day."*

This may seem obscure to include, but I like how even those seizing Peter and John did not feel like the job had to be finished and carried through as the day was winding down. What can wait until tomorrow?

As I read through the New Testament passages about evenings, it strikes me that Jesus was mentioned as teaching His disciples in the evenings rather than the masses. Perhaps He did teach the masses in the evenings, but there are several references to reclining, enjoying a meal, and a good teachable conversation with the disciples. This strikes me that evenings are for fixing our gaze inward into our own homes and those God has allowed us to share these mornings and evenings with. It is a drawing in, quieting, focusing our ministry on those closest to us, and a stopping of work.

Now, let's consider morning and learn from God's Word:

Genesis 19:27, *"Early the next morning Abraham got up and returned to the place where he had stood before the Lord."*

Genesis 20:8, *"Early the next morning Abimelek summoned all his officials, and when he told them all that had happened, they were very much afraid."*

Genesis 21:14, *"Early the next morning Abraham took some food and a skin of water and gave them to Hagar. He set them on her shoulders and then sent her off with the boy. She went on her way and wandered in the Desert of Beersheba."*

Genesis 22:3, *"Early the next morning Abraham got up and loaded his donkey. He took with him two of his servants and his son Isaac. When he had cut enough wood for the burnt offering, he set out for the place God had told him about."*

Mornings are for not only for action to begin but also obedience. This obedience did not start slow but early and big! Officials were summoned, journeys began, oaths taken/made, action on things God laid on their hearts and minds in the night and/or through dreams; lots more emotion and depth is communicated in the morning scenes—a going forth. There are numerous references that continue this theme.

Exodus 34:1-4, *"The Lord said to Moses, 'Chisel out two stone tablets like the first ones, and I will write on them the words that were on the first tablets, which you broke. Be ready in the morning, and then come up on Mount Sinai. Present yourself to me there on top of the mountain. No one is to come with you or be seen anywhere on the mountain; not even the flocks and herds may graze in front of the mountain.' So Moses chiseled out two stone tablets like the first ones and went up to Mount Sinai early in the morning, as the Lord had commanded him; and he carried the two stone tablets in his hands."*

I love the picture of being prepared for the next day. What is the important task for tomorrow that I can prepare for today? Set out the breakfast dishes? Get the coffee ready to start? Put the clothes in the washer so it is ready to start? Think ahead to meals?

Psalm 5:3, *"In the morning, Lord, You hear my voice; in the morning I lay my requests before you and wait expectantly."*

Psalm 88:13, *"But I cry to You for help, Lord; in the morning my prayer comes before You."*

Psalm 90:14, *"Satisfy us in the morning with Your unfailing love, that we may sing for joy and be glad all our days."*

Psalm 143:8, *"Let the morning bring me word of Your unfailing love, for I have put my trust in You. Show me the way I should go, for to You I entrust my life."*

Isaiah 33:2, *"Lord, be gracious to us; we long for You. Be our strength every morning, our salvation in time of distress."*

Isaiah 50:4, *"The Sovereign Lord has given me a well-instructed tongue, to know the word that sustains the weary. He wakens me morning by morning, wakens my ear like one being instructed."*

Mark 1:35, *"Very early in the morning, while it was still dark, Jesus got up, left the house and went away to a solitary place, where he prayed."*

Luke 21:38, *"…and all the people came early in the morning to hear Him at the temple."*

Morning is for spiritual nourishment. As I was reading over all of these and many, many more references to this idea, it reminded me of slow. Slowing our schedule, slowing my heart, etc. These words surrender, listen, obey, worship is really what morning is as described in these above verses. We surrender our day to Him, listen to His Word and obey it, and worship Him in it. It is a relying on His strength, a feeding on His Word, living it out before my children as a sacrifice of praise {worship} to Him. There is a quiet beauty about the early morning, a peace that hovers delicately; it is a time for strengthening, studying, and prayer.

Find a quiet spot and spend some time reflecting on what we just studied together in God's Word. You can use the following questions to spur on your time of reflection. I hope that all this practice at slowing will give you the confidence to keep at it!

Slow Journal:

Prayer One: Proverbs 3:17-18, *"Her ways are pleasant ways and all her paths are peace. She is a tree of life to those who take hold of her, those who hold her fast will be blessed."*

Write out a prayer of your own.

Prayer Two: Morning What do you like about your mornings at home? What is working? Is there anything not working about your mornings? Be specific.

Consider the patterns of mornings we have seen—nourishment, worship, beginning of work, doing the important things early, being prepared. Do these words stir up anything in you? Think and pray through what God has for your mornings. Praise Him for what is effective and working; seek Him for things that need to change.

Prayer Three: Evening What do you like about your evenings at home? What is working?

Is there anything not working about your evenings? Be specific. Consider the patterns we saw of evenings —slowing, quieting, nourishment, drawing in, ceasing of work, conversation, hymns, enjoying beauty together. Do these words stir up anything in you?

Think and pray through what God has for your evenings. Praise Him for what is effective and working; seek Him for things that need to change.

Gleaning Slow

Slow is a practice that we *glean* from here and there. We may adopt one small thing that helps us slow and, in turn, that may build into a second thing and so on. It strikes me that gleaning is slow; when you are picking up the leftovers around the edges of a field or taking what is left behind, it may take more work than getting the first pick. Learning to slow may be like that for many of us. It may be a natural desire, but it may not come naturally to step out of the fray and intentionally slow down.

Just as when gleaning a field or a fruit tree produce a higher yield on some days than others, so it is in our days and gleaning the habits of *slowing*. Learning to slow is not instant; sometimes we {I} fail at this desire, and it is a series of choices that lead us into a slower lifestyle. And, so we glean a little here ... a little there.

We study God's Word and read, *"Be still..."* We may see a sunset and feel a slowing, our children want us to sit and read books, or we sit and write a letter to a friend. In all of these ways, we are gathering slow one small moment at a time.

We can't heap it up in piles and save it for when we need it; it is simply something in the moment. Moments can add up to more moments and choices add up to more slowing choices; these are the ways to build slow.

All this reminds me, too, that slow is not without sacrifice or cost. We must give something else up in its place. Many times we are giving up hurry, stress, or tension, but sometimes there is a hard choice to sacrifice productivity, crossing things off the list, and knowing that there is a greater good being done in the not doing. Again, I am in no way encouraging slow to give up and shut down all expectations of accomplishing things.

Balance is key in so very many areas of life. We don't want to worship the list, but to rather have it serve us. We don't want to crave productivity so much that we are addicted to it. But, yes, there are things we must accomplish. We cannot become a slave of slow nor worship it; however, we can reap a blessing if we glean a little here and a little there.

Choosing Slow

Friends, slow is something we will have to seek out and choose purposefully. Slow often doesn't just happen in this day and age. With such a hustle-and-bustle society swarming around us from every direction, we must choose to step outside of the crazy hustle and be willing to be still.

Psalm 46:10, *"Be still and know that I am God."* That verse will forever remind me of a devotion I heard during my single working years. At a staff meeting, a member of the leadership team shared this verse and suggested reading it one word at a time, adding one word each time and pausing at the end of each line to let that sit and soak in.[3]

Be.

Be *still.*

Be still *and.*

Be still and *know.*

Be still and know *that.*

Be still and know that *I.*

Be still and know that I *am.*

Be still and know that I am *God.*

Completing this exercise will slow your heart and mind and cause you to pause and refocus. And it takes us back to that surrender. When you choose slow, you are saying no to something else. People might criticize you, they may not understand, but be still and know that He is God. God's got this. If this desire to slow is on your heart, I believe He will provide for you in that. And maybe it will be an opportunity to testify to others how God is working in your life.

Ideas for choosing slow:

- Be willing to look for slow pockets of time. Fifteen minutes can feel slow and reset your perspective sometimes just as much as a whole day of retreat and slow can.

- Slow Day – (see page 103)

- Something I love to do is pause at breakfast and go around the table, having everyone share one thing they would like to do that day. I add something in too, and we make an effort accomplish those things in the midst of our day. Take a walk, bake cookies, play a game, do

---

[3] Shared with permission from Craig Dunham; staff devotion was at Glen Eyrie Conference Center, Colorado Springs, CO.

a craft, watch a movie, sing a song, paint, garden… What is it for you?

Try one thing and practice it. After that, you can consider adding something else, but please don't try every idea you can think of all at once! I certainly don't want slow to be just another thing to do or try and squeeze in. I hope and pray even just an ounce of slow will work its way into the fabric of this tapestry called life to bless you and your family each day.

Simplify

If there is one mantra in our society that may possibly encourage slowing, it is this word *simplify*. But I'm not sure that what our culture promotes as simplify is truly simplicity.

I am one of those people who goes to a lot of trouble, and I get pleasure out of going to a lot of trouble. It is one of the ways I show love to and serve those around me. Cooking from scratch, coming up with a lovely table setting, moving the table outside so we can enjoy a new view, and beautifying spaces and activities and events are part of the fabric of who I am. To eliminate that would essentially be me saying to God that I don't want to be who He made me to be because I don't have time for it or it is too complicated.

Yet, just like so many things, simplicity is a choice. I can choose a simpler way sometimes and still maintain the essence of who God made me to be. When I have an idea of how I want something to be but it is falling at a very busy time, I want to take that idea and see what I can do to make it simpler in an effort to detour stress when possible.

Even though I may *want* to make a dessert from scratch for a coming invite, do I *have* to? Will it alter the event if I don't bring a homemade dessert? Not likely. However, if I push through and make that homemade dessert and wound someone around me with harsh and hurried words, will that alter our relationship? Quite likely. Do you see the difference?

I would rather stop by the grocery store and choose a dessert and have time to invest in one of my children or a special friend or family member. Remember, as we looked at above, slow chooses the things that really matter in life. People matter. Relationships matter. They matter for eternity, which is a big, big deal.

Being around people and investing in them is often far from simple. We still need healthy boundaries in order to keep peace within our homes and even to keep our relationships vibrant and healthy. Choose the better thing, and it will not be taken from you.

Talk to God

Remember, we are not in this alone! I love the Psalms because it seems that David is such a real person, and he shares from the hard reality of life situations that threaten to overtake and overwhelm.

When you are in this spot, come before God. Talk to Him. Share your heart. He longs for these times of sweet communication with you. Write a prayer, go for a walk and talk to Him in your heart, drive in your car alone and talk to Him out loud. You can pray anytime, anywhere, any way. Just please remember that He is listening and He wants to bless you. He has your best in mind.

Pick a Psalm and read it, personalize it with your own name and the details that are present for you. Focus specifically on God's promises and watch for God's power at work to strengthen you and encourage.

Slow Day

During recent years, we have found ourselves in Colorado every summer for about a month visiting my parents. One summer, I found myself at different times sitting on the porch just to watch my children play, crochet a dish rag or read a book.

This was the summer that God was planting an idea in my heart. He was forming the beginning of *Slow Day*. Not once a year but once a week—not to cease work but just to *s l o w*.

When we get home from vacation and anticipate getting back to school, back to chores, meal planning, and so many life details that need attention, this idea beckons and invites.

Take one day a week to slow the pace. Stay home as much of that day as possible, sitting on the porch, reading books, having tea, *slowing*. We will still have school and do laundry and need to eat, but we can slow down the other minutes and hours. We can lie on the couch and read books all afternoon if we want to, do puzzles or play games, sit on the porch swing, and sip lemonade, etc.

In the beginning, I felt inexperienced about how this idea of slow would work and what it would look like during real life. If the idea is compelling and you are willing to trust God, trust Him to help make it work.

I like this verse in that it reminds me to let others go on ahead of me and be willing to move more slowly if that is what suits my family the best. Jacob is the one speaking while on the way to meet his brother Esau.

Genesis 33:14, *"So let my lord go on ahead of his servant, while I move along slowly at the pace of the flocks and herds before me and the pace of the children, until I come to my lord in Seir."*

Why Slow Day?

This question takes me back a few years to when Emily (our oldest) was just four and the world of opportunities seemed to be opening before her of things to get involved in: Awana, Children's Choir at church and school. Have you realized how many commitments are available to our sweet four-year-olds? It is a magical age in the realm of over-scheduling, and suddenly we are faced with decisions of how much to be involved in, how often to go, and so on.

Especially since this was my oldest child and we were doing all of this for the first time, it was (and obviously still is) a big struggle for me to think about the time spent out of our home if we did all or even some of these things.

We decided on one thing at church and one more physical activity: Children's Choir and Ballet. That felt doable and good; we had to say no to other good things, but we did that. We also had two children under four, so they were a big consideration in these decisions.

Fast forward a few years, and we had three who were over age four. Now all of these opportunities were tripled. Every year we have re-evaluated our time commitments to see if we are stewarding our time well. As our children crossed this magic age four and the opportunities were and still are multiplying, it was a constant battle for me to not be too busy. Even as a homeschooling family, the opportunities are endless—field trips, play dates, park invites, classes, lessons, and more. We live in an age of opportunity for sure. We can do anything, anytime, at any age.

What exactly are we teaching our children in this? That the world is theirs for the taking, that it is being held out to them on a silver platter? I will admit that we still do a lot and we are still busy, but I know if we had not been thinking about this each year, we would be exponentially more committed and involved in more than we could handle.

I am an introvert, which means being alone energizes me, and peace and quiet and slow energize me. I think this is where my struggle begins. I am in a season of noise both audible, visual, and

scheduling-wise. In order to maintain my balance, I have to have some slowing, some quiet, and some peace to recharge me from the noisy season I am in.

As anyone who has young children, had young children at one point or has even been around young children knows—peace, quiet and slow are not exactly their mode of operation! Not only is it healthy and needed for me—I have to believe it is good for my children to learn how to live slower and more quietly. That doesn't mean I constantly walk around shushing them—it means that we strive for more of a quietness of life and heart.

What is Slow Day?

Initially when this idea presented itself, it began as a day we could stay home and have no outside commitments. A day we were able to slow each week.

When thinking along these lines, the natural next thought was okay, when would I do that and what day would be good for that? Honestly, I got stuck here already. I really didn't want Monday or Friday to be our Slow Day because they were on the edge of the weekend and I was afraid we'd lose our rhythm. Tuesday was out because we had homeschool community group that day. Thursday was ballet and soccer, and Wednesday was Children's Choir at church.

Oh boy. Yes, we needed Slow Day, but how to fit in? Ahem.

I began to talk to my mom about all of this. We were at their house for our summer visit, and I needed to process and figure this out. It bothered and embarrassed me that I could not figure out when to fit a Slow Day in.

We started talking through our schedule, and my mom wisely suggested Wednesday. It was in the middle of the week—perfect! It was the day after our community school day—needed! David does take our children to choir at church, but I stay home. I was initially trying really hard to make it a day we didn't need to go anywhere, but my wonderful mom helped me see that this really could work and be a good solution. Now that the day was figured out, what does Slow Day really look like?

My next thoughts were that my production could not cease on Slow Day, for that would just leave me feeling behind other days, and I would struggle to keep this routine because it was setting me up for failure. So the first important note about what Slow Day is would be that it is not a ceasing of work. We still have school; I still do laundry. Our basic routine is the same as any other day.

Slow Day is a call to *slow*. It is a day to regroup and pull in. It's a day I can say yes to other things like taking a walk, picnics, making breakfast special, playing a game, and longer reading times. It is a day we get out and enjoy nature, a day for tea parties, and, yes, making lunch special too! I don't try to create extra work for myself, but I do try to see how I can use what is available. I can take the time to put the breakfast muffins on a cake stand or pull out striped straws or something fun and simple like that. If that doesn't light your fire, skip it and choose something else!

Okay, so Slow Day is slowing down enough to say yes, choosing to stay home, a big white space of open bliss on the calendar. Now, how do we make this work in our home?

How Do You Start Slow Day?

So how exactly do we do Slow Day? Of course, this will look different in every family. I can only speak from our family and inside these walls what Slow Day is like. Hopefully sharing what my family does will give you ideas to implement in your own family!

An important note at this moment is that we have set home hours. I unplug our phone every morning and have a note on the door that we don't answer before 2:00 p.m.

I usually try to fix a hot breakfast on Slow Day—that is a slowing for sure! It doesn't have to be long and complicated though: muffins or leftover sausage casserole. Making a pot of hot tea is simple enough and still appreciated and slowing.

Our morning routine is really very unchanged. We start by reading aloud during breakfast, brushing teeth, making beds, and getting ready for the day. We start school and all is as usual. Sometimes we may go for a walk before or after school. We may go pick up the fallen magnolia cones that are all over the driveway for ten minutes or tend the garden.

As with breakfast, I try to fix something out of the ordinary and warm and slowing for lunch. And, just as with breakfast, it does not have to take a lot of time. Leftover chicken noodle soup from the night before with freshly toasted grilled cheese, leftover quiche from a prayer shower with a little salad, really whatever feels right and like it would work. Frequently we have a picnic or eat on the screened-in porch or go for a walk. We read and linger. Do a puzzle or play a game or bake something together.

Slow Day is like any new habit or routine; it takes practice and trying things to find out what works. A simple bit of planning has made this exponentially more successful for us. Planning ahead is the

key to success for so many areas in my life. When I am working ahead, it is building in slow for a future day.

Planning is such a blessing because if you think about it, planning helps by removing the last-minute stress and worry of being in a hurry. I won't be standing in the kitchen at 12:32 p.m. with hungry children running around me asking what is for lunch; I will be ready and prepared.

Even though a day to slow and pull in is what I'm describing, I still plan for this day. I don't make a lot of preparations in advance but just have a general plan and guide. Of course, there is a place for spontaneity and we still have room for that if it comes up. I'd rather be spontaneous and toss out something else I'd planned than have to scramble around and figure something out in a moment of hurry.

Slow Day has been a huge blessing in our home; it is my favorite day of the week. I'm still learning and still wanting to implement more slow, but this has blessed us where we are in the learning and growing.

God Created the Original Slow Day

Slow Day is not intended to take the place of the Sabbath. That is a day created and set aside by God for worship and rest. Remember, Slow Day is not a day to cease work. Life must go on, and homes and families will still need caring for.

I simply love that God set a beautiful example for us in slowing. Resting. Taking a pause. One quick glance at the Creation account will show any reader that on the seventh day, He rested. We spent quite a bit of time studying this passage already, so we don't need to revisit it. It encourages and blesses my heart, though, to see how He sets the example for us in slowing.

Slow Journal

How does the idea of implementing a Slow Day sound to you?

Is there something about it that makes it appealing and/or seem unrealistic?

Pray and ask God and talk to your husband. Is this something that could be a blessing to your family?

Spend some time thinking about what day would be a good fit for you home/family. Jot down some thoughts about what Slow Day might look like for you.

Slowing Stress: Resting in Him

If there is one thing I think my family would like more than anything else, it is that I would not get *stressed*. I mean, have you ever had your little seven-year-old boy come up to you and rub your arm and say, *"I'm sorry you're stressed, mama…"* Oh.my.

Here's the thing, I don't *want* to be stressed. I don't want to allow myself to go down that road, yet it comes so easily, doesn't it? I'm not alone, right?

I've been thinking about this a lot: What are my triggers for stress? How does stress show a lack of trust in God? How does stress affect myself and my family?

Stress vs. Slow

First, let's consider what stress is and what slow is. How does stress vs. slow affect us? What does it bring? What are its side-kicks?

Here are some I thought of, and feel free to add your own to the list:

Stress	Slow
Wearying	Comforting
Anxious	Peaceful
Draining	Refreshing
Unhealthy	Healthy
Repelling	Restorative/Inviting
Burdensome	Freeing
Heavy	Light
Takes	Gives
Angry/Irritated	Kind/Joyful
Tiring	Restful
Caught up in what is going wrong	Values what is most important
Hard to honor God, easy to sin	Follows God's example
Control-seeking	Life-Giving; Flexible

Where would you put yourself on this chart right now? Jot down a few thoughts about that; take time to process it. Why would you put yourself on that side? What do you think is contributing to that right now? Pray for wisdom to seek changes you can make to help in troublesome areas.

God's Plan for Stress Management

I bet you can guess who came to my mind when I began to think of stress in Scripture and looking for a biblical example that we could follow. Mary and Martha!

We've already spent quite a bit of time studying Mary, but we're going to do it again. Not referencing our notes on what we already studied but just looking at it new and fresh this time. We humans can be very slow learners, and I'm so grateful for God's patience to us in this process.

Look at Luke 10:38-42. List everything you learn about each of these sisters below:

Martha	Mary
Opened her home to Jesus and His disciples	Martha's sister
Distracted by preparations	Sat at Jesus' feet

Quickly, you can see that Martha chose stress and Mary chose slow. Mary was surrendered, she listened, she obeyed, she worshipped. Not only did Jesus praise Mary for this choice, His praise seems like an invitation to Martha. Martha sounds like me – she likes productivity, she loves God, but can have trouble in the heat of the moment making wise, God-pleasing attitude choices. She is an over-achiever and can get frustrated when others don't appreciate her drive for quality or presentation.

It is hard to sit still. It is hard to slow. Believe me, I know it takes practice. I've been at it for several years, and I fail all the time and stumble and struggle.

What is it about Mary's attitude and approach that call to you? What part of her demeanor do you find difficult to implement or choose?

Choosing stress almost seems like a non-choice. Stress heads straight for us at high speed and seems to hit us without knowing what happened. Yet the first step for us needs to be that we see it coming and head straight for that "one thing" that Jesus shows us how much we need.

Practical Stress-Avoiding Ideas

As much as I love a simple answer like Jesus gave of just choosing that one thing, sometimes I need a little hand-holding to get from point a to point b. Are you with me?

I started looking through my Bible for some ideas of ways to manage stress. When I find myself in that moment where stress is threatening to overtake me, what can I turn to that will practically help me in these moments where I am on the edge and desperately wanting to choose God's way.

Here are some Scriptures for you to look up. Read the verse, write it out, jot down a few thoughts, whatever God brings to mind or that you feel would be of benefit to you.

- Seek help from the Lord. 2 Chronicles 20:4

- Be still. Psalm 46:10

- Give thanks. 2 Corinthians 9:8-10

- Focus on that which is true and good. Philippians 4:8

- Remember God's promises. Joshua 1:9

- Take courage. 2 Chronicles 15:8

- Sing to the Lord. 2 Chronicles 20:21

- Cast anxiety on Him. 1 Peter 5:7

A few other simple, practical ideas:

- Sit quietly.

- Take a short walk {even to the mailbox!}

- Breathe deeply several times.

- Surrender, Listen, Obey, Worship.

- Rest.

- Put a drop of lavender and peppermint on your wrist and take a deep breath.

- Pray.

- Sit on your porch.

- Sing a worship song.

- Put on some worship music.

- Don't run late, plan ahead a bit, or start a few minutes early to avoid the last-minute haste.

Write out a set of index cards with verses that speak peace, calm, and slow to you. Keep them in a handy spot to pull out during these times where you are on the verge of losing it. See Appendix C for cards you can cut out and hole punch to put on a ring.

Choosing Slow Instead of Stress

I woke up one morning with a lengthy list ahead of me for the day; it was one of those days where I was overwhelmed before it started. Instead of jumping up and getting going, I found myself sort of paralyzed by the hurry and hustle that was waiting. I browsed Instagram and read a couple of blogs and found myself lost in the inspiration of beautiful moments of life. Beautiful photography does that to me—it draws me in and beckons me to join in. And it is restful and soothing just as hurry rushes in and steals those things. I decided to notice the beauty around me and love on those in my home instead of getting tense and hurrying them along to more productivity.

Just doing simple homey things like fixing breakfast and tending my garden and praying fed my spirit and blessed my home much more than marking things off my to-do list. Truthfully, our morning went much more smoothly and I got more done than I could have imagined two hours earlier. I chose peace instead of fast-paced.

It wasn't even a really decisive move; it was gradual and felt more like choosing to breathe instead of suffocate. And suddenly the things waiting for my day felt much more manageable than heavy.

Taking one step at a time...

Taking time to notice that I loved seeing my enamelware dishes in the drying rack waiting to be put away. Taking the time to try a new recipe for Emily. To cut flowers lingering on hydrangea bushes. Time to set a pretty table.

Do I have time? Yes and no, but I only get this amount of time once for today. I don't want to spend it in stress and with tension. I want to choose slow. How often do I have this crisis of decision? I want to choose slow, and yet stress creeps in so very easily and is quite bossy in taking over frequently.

As I have remembered time and time again, I will never ever regret that I took time to cut flowers and lovingly make and serve breakfast with beauty. Even on this side of things, I am pretty certain that I will regret choosing hurry or allowing stress to take over my day.

I love this from She Reads Truth:

Give Thanks in Stress[4]

Lord, make us lie down in green pastures, Lord, lead us beside still waters, Lord, restore our souls.

We confess that we choose rush over rest, we choose busy over best. We bow down to expectations and worship our lists. Forgive us, Lord. You are steadfast. Thank you. You give us rest. Thank you. You slow our step and calm our hearts and allow us to sit at your feet. Thank you. Thank you. Thank you.

We will praise you in the noise, we will praise you in the stress; for you remain unchanged, and we are found in you.

Amen.

Slow Journal

Here is your chance to process anything that stood out to you in this section on practical slowing of life. Is there anything that seems hard or impossible about slowing down? Is there anything that seems particularly simple or easy?

If you were to choose one thing to focus on to begin slow in your home and family, what would it be and how can you implement it?

What are the areas in your life that are causing stress more than others? What needs to go or even just change?

---

[4] Give Thanks in Stress is reprinted with permission from She Reads Truth; www.shereadstruth.com. Prayer written by Amanda Bible Williams, November 21, 2014.

Slow Holidays

If there is one time a mama can really lose it, it's when senses and expectations are heightened – holidays! And to be honest, I'm the one with the expectations most of the time. How can we possibly enjoy these special times when we are the ones who must make them happen?

Please hear this: I have not perfected this! These are ideas, and I am preaching to myself as much as anything else. There are a few holidays that I am really good at slowing at, but I can get just as caught up in the busy and bustle as anyone.

We happen to be a family who likes quiet holidays at home. If you prefer inviting friends over or accepting invitations, you'll want to adapt slowing at holidays to fit your family style. I'm just going to toss out some ideas that we love and hope that they trigger an idea or thought you might be able to implement in slowing to more fully enjoy the next holiday!

Choose Simple Fun at Home

If I had to solidify what makes the following ideas simpler and slower, it would be that we have fun at home. I can pull off a fun evening at home pretty easily just by setting the mood myself and making it fun. My kids are older now, and they've gotten into the fun of the planning and pulling off too. If you keep a pack of glow sticks, some party napkins, and plan ahead for a fun thing or two at each holiday, you'll be all set for a fun family memory opportunity.

Consider Your Priorities

As a holiday approaches, spend a few minutes thinking about any particular details that will apply to your family. If something is sounding stressful before it has even arrived, brainstorm some ways to bring slow and peace to your home before the chaos erupts.

What is most important to you about the coming holiday?

What pieces of the celebration are up to you or under your control? What things are not? Are they negotiable?

If you had to pick one thing that you'd most like to accomplish or enjoy together on that holiday, what would it be? How can you break it up into chunks a few days in advance to make it more doable and enjoyable for all?

What Others Think

Here is a big one. I have to get away from worrying about what others will think about what we choose to do for a holiday and why we do or do not do that. If we don't meet the status quo for traditional foods served or activities to plan and attend, why does it matter what anyone else thinks if our family is happy with the arrangement?

Sometimes More is Just More

A good reminder is that we can't do it all. I don't do it all. If it looks like I do it all, look behind all that and see what I am not doing. Even though holidays are ripe with fun opportunities and events, sometimes more is just more and not really blessing my family through hustle and hurry. If I pick and choose a couple of special things or rather focus on special traditions our family has, won't that be a better use of time and energy and a stress-saver during holidays?

Let Pinterest Serve You

When a holiday is approaching and you want a pretty decoration or free printable, go for it! I'm all for creating and planning beauty for our celebrations. In fact, one thing that makes a holiday seem like a holiday to me is having time to do something creative.

If I have already researched a couple of ideas and made sure I have the supplies on hand in advance, I can enjoy the peaceful slow of creating something to bless my family and our celebration without driving everyone crazy.

Give yourself permission to not have to come up with something amazing and unique that you designed and thought of yourself. Let yourself enjoy the creativity of someone else and grab that free printable that you can have printed and framed in a mere two minutes.

Let yourself be inspired and have that creative spark fueled, but don't let it consume you in your pursuit of a perfect holiday. Look at the holiday and celebration through the eyes of your family and try to see what they see. What sort of example are you setting for your children? What values are you lifting up or not?

Bite-Sized Chunks

I love to plan for holidays, so this comes naturally to me, but even if it isn't easy for you, you may find this or some variation of it to be a benefit.

Two to three weeks before a holiday, I like to jot down a list of things I'd enjoy doing, making, and trying. It could be a recipe I want to experiment with or even menu ideas for what I hope to serve or something for the table I'd love to make.

Once you have a guide, consider how you can take little nibbles at that over the next couple of weeks before the holiday arrives. I think it is especially fun to have decorations made and ready to go before the day so that when it arrives, I can enjoy the slow fun of just setting a beautiful table and relishing the process.

If this appeals to you, you might like something like Organized Christmas {www.organizedchristmas.com}, where you can find great checklists and printables to help organize your holiday celebration. The lists encourage you to do smaller chunks of projects weeks in advance including putting food in your freezer, buying your stamps early, and more. Of course, the goal is that you will have those things done and out of the way and more room in your schedule to relax and enjoy the beauty of those days.

You can apply this Organized Christmas principle to any holiday.

Leave Room for Spontaneity

Allowing some wiggle room in your schedule will not only keep you feeling calmer and more at peace, it will allow you that freedom to be spontaneous. We have made some fun memories with the simplest of ingredients this way because we said yes to spontaneity Here's a non-holiday example:

Recently my husband came home from work with some extra sub sandwiches left from feeding those who were working an event. The sandwiches were already made, and it was like they were just begging to be taken on a picnic. When I opened the bags, there were also little bags of chips enclosed.

I unwrapped the sandwiches, cut them in half, and re-wrapped them with a little slip of the wrapper and some twine. Some instant lemonade and a few cookies sitting on our counter were added, and we had a lovely picnic at a local beachfront (See picture on page 81.).

It took almost no time to pull off, but we made a beautiful memory on a Sunday evening as our children dipped toes and buckets into water, we watched dolphins at play farther out, and the sunset cast a glorious glow over all we could see.

Monica Wilkinson

This is true not just at holidays, but any time we are so scheduled that there is no room for embracing slow opportunities just dropped in our laps, we will miss so very much.

Consider the Blessings

When considering Slow Holidays or even just celebrating the everyday joy of life, will you ever regret slowing? Will you ever regret hurrying or failing to slow? How will those answers affect your life and the lives of those you share your home with each day?

Consider the blessings of slowing and ponder how you can choose to celebrate alongside slow when the next holiday or everyday moment approaches.

Your Slow Season

Slow is so different for every home, every family, and every life. If you choose to make that jaunt into slow and let it calm your days and heart, it will look different than when I do that. And there is also a real possibility that if you are around me, you might not think my life is slow enough to talk about slow so much.

Thoughts creep in and make me wonder what you are thinking of me, and I try to push them out. So before they take over, I have this realization that this is my slow. This is the slow that works for us right now. It may not work next week or next year or in ten years, but it is how we slow right now.

You have a reality like that. Slow that works for me doesn't work exactly the same for you. Only you and I each know our own reality, what life is like daily. Only you or I with God together know how to slow that reality down. There is no one-size-fits-all recipe for slow. Not every family will consider this a priority or even something they need. Maybe life is too slow for them and they need more community. There is even the negative side of slow—dilly dallying, laziness, lack of common sense.

Let slow slip into your home and heart in your very own way, like slipping on clothes that are just your style. Let slow wrap you up in a peace that frantic makes impossible. Be you. Slow down. Breathe.

Slowing with Littles

I love the question that was asked on an Instagram photo I posted about how to slow with kids around. It really got me thinking about how we do this slow even though I have three children

with lots of energy around me all the time. We homeschool, and they are literally with me all day, every day.

Model Slow

The first thought that came to mind when I considered this question was that I have to be willing to show and tell my kids what slow looks like and what it is. Do my kids ever see me sitting still, reading a book, crocheting, or playing a game with them?

If my children never see me sit still, how will they learn to value and understand that this is not only okay but healthy for our well-being in a fast-paced, busy world?

You can begin modeling slow by yourself before you attempt to engage your whole family in this practice if you choose. Try to sit still and quietly, even when your children can see you, for even ten or fifteen minutes.

Inviting more of your family to join you can come as you have gained a peaceful countenance in slowing and learning this practice of being still and not filling every moment with something to engage ourselves or our children in.

One idea I've reaped benefits on in modeling slow is pointing out little treasures in God's creation. Since my children were tiny, I've pointed out the song of a bird, a nest, the beauty of an almost-blooming flower, and the glory of a sunset. Now it thrills my heart when we are in the dentist's office and a little hand will tap my arm and say there is a bird at the window or that the light streaming through the trees is dreamy and can we please chase the sunset?

Start Small

I think this slowing and creating slow beauty for my family comes easily to me. In fact, I crave it. So in many ways, I think my kids have grown up in this slow mentality and lifestyle. But what if you are just joining the slow team? How would you model it? And what if you are not good at slow?

Start somewhere and start small. Invite your children to sit on the porch with you for five minutes. Read a story aloud, look at what is going on in nature, pray together, have a mini tea party with water in fancy cups. Anything just to slow together. Next time, try ten minutes or even fifteen. Consider what is realistic for your family's personality.

Quiet Time

I'm an introvert, so quiet is not only something nice to have, it is essential to my ability to think and get through the long haul of homeschooling and mothering. But let's face it – I have three children and my life is pretty noisy! With that in mind, I've tried to build some quiet into our routines at home.

I usually get up and have my Bible Quiet Time before anyone else is up, so this reference to quiet time is different than that. Once my children outgrew the idea of naps, we began quiet time. It is a time set aside after lunch and playing outside where my main rule is that it is quiet. I set a timer so everyone knows how much time is left and won't feel the need to interrupt the quiet to ask! The amount of time varies by what else we have going on, but I strive for no less than 30 minutes and no more than 60 minutes. I've found 45 minutes is our most successful time.

When little hands and bodies got restless during quiet time, I came up with a quiet time schedule. It includes activities for each child that change every day so they always have something new or fun to do. I keep a few items on a shelf in the closet that are typically only pulled out during quiet time. Activities we have enjoyed are: drawing, reading, having a turn on the iPad, Lite Brite, magnetic dolls, puzzles, playing blocks or Legos, and Play-Doh.

My children are not allowed to play together during quiet time. They all have to be in separate places and must occupy themselves quietly. I sit in the living room on my favorite small couch and usually read and sometimes even fall asleep. Because the timer is set, it is a natural alarm clock for me when that time is over and we've all had some refreshing down time that is quiet.

There is value in learning the beauty of quiet and spending time alone. It can be uncomfortable to be quiet around each other, and we can want to fill that silence sometimes, so there can be great wisdom in finding comfort in quiet.

When bed time is getting stressful and clean up is a repeated problem in the evening, I've also been known to implement a second quiet time in the evening. This is for after everyone is ready for bed and we all bring something quiet to the living room, where we spend 15-30 minutes together quietly. Reading and drawing are the two most popular activities in the evening. It really brings the energy of the day down to a get-ready-for-bed level that is peaceful and calming.

Family Fun Hour

I already told you I like FlyLady and have found her cleaning ideas and routines helpful in managing our home. I mentioned one of my favorite things is the Home Blessing Hour. It is a weekly hour where you bless your home by taking care of six ten-minute chores that need to be done. My children and I do this Home Blessing Hour together every Wednesday, which also happens to be our Slow Day.

Something I came up with as a reward for this Home Blessing Hour teamwork is Family Fun Hour. When we have finished our chores, I will let each of my children choose one thing they want us to do together that afternoon: play a game, bake something, or do an art project. We will usually spend about twenty minutes on each of the three activities chosen allowing us to spend that Family Fun Hour together doing things they want to do.

Sometimes I will have something I'd like to do with them as well like go for a walk or paint. When we have four things, we just spend around fifteen minutes on each activity, and it still works out to be about an hour. This has been a fun way to get us to think about things we'd like to do together and to practice playing together. It's also a great way for us as a family to support and enjoy the choices of others in our family.

Brainstorm Slow

Consider opening the conversation at the dinner table about what slow means to each family member. You could go on to share what you are learning and maybe even some of your vision for slow in your home and family.

Get ideas from your family on what slowing down as a family would look like to you, keeping in mind your schedule and unique family preferences. If your children are very tiny, they will grow up in what you model and say about slow. If they are older, you can get their input on what this could look like for your family.

What if My Kids Are in School?

Some of you are probably thinking, but I don't homeschool! My kids are in school and then we have homework and dinner and bedtime routines and there is no time to slow! You are right that slow will look different for you than it does for me. But that can be true of hundreds of situations and scenarios aside from schooling choices.

As I've said earlier, I will say again: slow will look different for many different kinds of families. Could you pick one evening a week that you have Slow Evening rather than Slow Day? Stay home. Make something special for dinner, play a game together, or listen to beautiful music and be together.

Please hear me say that slow should not complicate your life but be a blessing to it.

Maybe you could pick one weekend a month where you don't have a lot of extra commitments and call that your Slow Weekend. Or even just a Slow Morning on Saturdays with a little extra beauty and care tucked into the start of your day.

Serve breakfast in bed with a little jar of flowers or berries gently placed on one side. Fix your kids lunches so they don't have to in the mornings and use that time to serve them instead.

Do you have an extra thirty minutes to spend on your drive or walk home from school? Pack a little after-school snack and stop at a park to enjoy slowing together, talking about your day, and soaking in a little of God's beauty that surrounds you.

On your way to the library to gather research for a paper or project, could you spare a few minutes to stop for a treat? These little moments add up and create a life of slow even if you only have a few moments to work with. You can still choose and cultivate slow.

How about a bedtime candlelight cookie picnic or a candlelit bath? I've done this before when my kids come home from choir on Wednesday evenings. I will set the coffee table with some treat and little cups of milk, light a few candles, and have something to read them set out and ready. Bath time is something we have to make time for; how can you make it a little more special and model slow by showing how you are caring for and serving your family?

We Are in a Busy Season of Life

This feeling applies to nearly everyone who could possibly pick up these words and read through them. Some of us are busier than others, sometimes by choice and sometimes by the path God has us on right now.

In writing all of the above ideas, I know that you are very busy. You may feel too busy to slow down, or you may feel like if you slow down you will somehow lose your momentum and never be able to get it back again.

I get it; I've had some of these thoughts myself. But I can honestly say that I have never once regretted my choices of slowing, and I most certainly have regretted moments of rush and hurry where my voice gets harsher and less gracious.

Slow doesn't have to happen every day or even every week. I will say it again: *slow will be a blessing when it is a good fit for you and your family.* Think small, but choose some way to slow together and take that deep breath and remember why you are so blessed to have the life that you do.

Praise God for the season He has you in and ask for wisdom and guidance in anything that can or should go from your schedule. Filling our lives with good things is only great if it is what God thinks is best for us. Let's look for His best!

Be a Slow Blessing

After many busy life scenarios, I realize there is also the possibility that life feels too slow for you. You may think you have plenty of time to slow but really almost too much of it.

May I suggest that you ask God how you can be a blessing of slow to someone else?

To the mother who can't even think straight at the grocery store with all her littles underfoot, take her dinner, watch her sweets while she shops, or bring her a few goodies from the farmer's market.

To the caregiver who is immersed in doctor appointments and what symptoms are next, offer the slow blessing of friendship and kindness. Call, send a card, or leave a treat on her front porch.

How can you be a slow blessing to one of your grown children? To your pastor's family? To those you come into contact with daily or even a neighbor?

Can you take time to pray, send notes, serve, come alongside, encourage? I daresay there are scores of needs around us that could benefit from a slow blessing like you. Pray and ask God to make you a blessing of slow and to show you who He wants you to invest in. May He be glorified!

Slow Inspiration

Hopefully you've actively read and taken to heart some of the ideas on slow presented here, and now you may be wondering how to start. This is one of my favorite things to do: celebrate the every day! I hope you will see that choosing slow does not need to be nor should it be complicated. It should naturally fit in as part of your family and be easy to execute! Here are some ideas of slow things to do together as a family to create memories together and enjoy slowing:

- Have a tea party on a quilt in your yard or on the floor of your living room.

- Go for a picnic. Try a breakfast or dessert picnic!

- Read aloud.

- Play a game or have a family movie night with snacks.

- Bake something and deliver to a friend who needs cheering.

- Sit on your porch, each with your own book or quiet slow activity.

- Garden.

- Enjoy what you live close to.

- Go to a new park as a family.

- Watch a sunset.

- Draw or do an art project together while listening to peaceful music.

- Go for a walk.

- Camp out in the living room.

- Serve others together as a family.

- Cut flowers or branches from your yard and leave on the porch of a friend or neighbor to cheer them.

- Write letters or make cards.

- Heat a quilt in the dryer to warm a cold love in your home.

- Serve breakfast in bed.

- Be spontaneous. Make a new Family Tradition!

- Create surprises.

- Celebrate the ordinary.

- Look for fun and thankfulness all around you.

- Chase beauty.

- Invite others to join slowing with you.

- Go for a scenic drive.

- Go for a bike ride together.

- Be in the same room together even if you are all doing different things.

- Look at the stars.

- Be a tourist in your own hometown.

- Have your children put on a puppet show or little program of their choosing one evening.

- Listen to the ideas of those in your home and when you can, allow time to make those things happen.

- Learn something new together.

PART FOUR
Where is God in Slow?

When I was digging deeper into my study of slow and struggled to find much that included God, I turned to His Word to see where the word *slow* appeared in Scripture. I hope you will be blessed by studying these verses along with me!

At the beginning of each section, I will list the overall section of Scripture to study. I will break it down by smaller chunks and share a few thoughts plus some questions for personal reflection within each section.

Exodus 3:1-12:42

Moses is speaking here about how he is slow of speech and tongue. God has asked him to go to and help deliver the Israelites from Egypt.

Exodus 3:1-4:

- Moses is curious about the burning bush and goes to check it out. He hears a call and his response, *"Here I am,"* is a surrendering to be available to God's plan. His surrender continues gradually through the passage. Actually it seems that Moses goes in and out of being willing to surrender. Not only that, Moses was listening. He *heard* God's voice and slowed enough to quiet the outside things of life and hear God.

- Moses also worshipped; he took off his sandals, *"for the place where you are is holy."* He adopted a different posture before God; less of Himself and more of God.

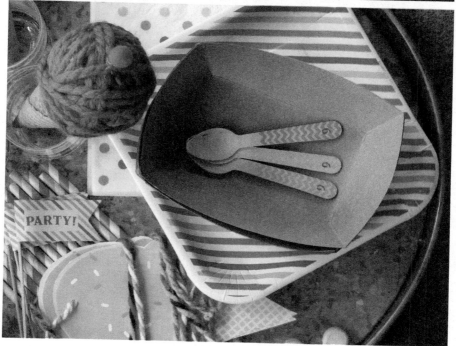

In what ways is God trying to get your attention?

Do you need to choose slow to be able to listen to Him?

Is there something God is asking you to surrender to Him?

What is your response to God? Are you willing to be made willing?

How does your response worship God {or not}?

Exodus 3:7-22:

- God has given Moses an assignment, a job to do, and it sounds overwhelming to Moses. Based on his response in verse 11, it is similar to when we are overwhelmed and we wonder how we will get it done. Look at God's response in verse 12, *"I will be with you!"*

- God reassures, equips, and enables us to obey His will. Moses questions God again and again, and God is so very patient with Moses.

- God gave Moses specific steps to follow and an orderly plan.

I can really relate with Moses in his feeling of being inadequate and overwhelmed with the task ahead. So often I feel inadequate. But I love that God comes right along behind and affirms Moses with a promise and truth that He is with us.

Is there something in your life right now that you are feeling inadequate and/or overwhelmed in?

How does the promise that God is with you bring courage, strength, and peace?

How can you walk forward in confidence knowing God is with you, knowing you are listening to and obeying something He has asked of you?

What is the next step you need to take? If you don't know yet, rest in God to show you in His timing and way. But if He has laid out a plan for you and you know it, what are you going to do about it?

Exodus 4:1-17:

- Look at the back-and-forth of the surrender and control. Moses is obviously struggling with this calling. One thing here that jumps out as slow to me is a heart at peace. I can't be at peace when I am wrestling like this.

Can you think of a time that you were struggling to surrender to God?

How can choosing a heart of surrender bring peace?

Exodus 4:18-23:

- Moses is not slow to obey. This is the time for action! When we have a mission from God, we should not delay in obeying!

Remember when we talked about obeying all the way, right away, with a happy heart? Think of how this blesses God our heavenly Father when we obey this way. Put yourself in Moses's place and think of what you might have been thinking, experiencing, explaining, etc.

Exodus 4:24-26:

- Moses had been slow to obey God in circumcising his son. We see here the hovering consequences of his slow obedience.

Think of a time you were slow to obey. What were the consequences? Or if you have had an experience with a child being slow to obey, think of how it hurt your heart and consider your heavenly Father and how He feels when we are slow.

Slow is not a bad word, but it can have negative connotations and side effects. List some of those here.

Exodus 4:27-31:

- There is beauty in this picture of Moses sharing with Aaron and then with both of them together sharing with the people of Israel. Moses and Aaron were surrendered to God; they were living less of themselves and their own agenda, and they were carrying out God's orders. Worship is surrender.

How is worship a form of surrender?

How do you see beauty in openly and honestly sharing what God is doing in and through you? Do you find it hard to remain humble in this circumstance? Do you genuinely seek God's glory?

As you consider this account of Moses, how do you see surrender, listening, obedience, and worship?

Exodus 5:1-5:

- Now we see the opposite of slow in looking at Pharaoh. Pharaoh shows us:

    o   A hardened heart

    o   A prideful heart

    o   Disobedience

    o   Rejection of God

- It is the exact opposite of what we are pursuing by choosing a heart of slow before God. But there is value in looking at the other side. We can be encouraged in choosing the right way, choosing God's way, and having a soft heart before God.

Do you struggle with any of the things we see modeled in Pharaoh? A hard heart? Pride? Disobedience? Rejecting God?

Please take a minute to talk to God about whatever you just wrote down. Is there something to confess? Seek forgiveness for? Ask for help in? Turn from and choose differently?

Is there anything in your life that you are not listening to God in right now? Where is your heart hard? Friend, I urge you to commit that to God and allow Him to mold and shape you for His glory and your good!

Exodus 5:6-23:

- When we desire to live with a heart of slow, there will be opposition! It is seen here in these verses. Pharaoh made the work harder and more strenuous. The people were beaten, harshly spoken to, and treated badly. We may experience great struggle in slowing--criticism and the efforts of evil will be diligent in busyness and discouragement. We, like the Israelites, may be tempted to try to place blame. But Moses sets a better example for us in going to God for help.

What kind of opposition have you endured for making choices pleasing to God?

How can you thank God in the midst of that knowing that you were choosing what is right?

Think of some ways you can turn to God during opposition rather than casting blame.

Exodus 6:1-8:

- God continues in His pursuit of slow:

    o   Surrender to His plan

    o   Listen to His voice

    o   Obey His will

    o   Worship as the result

- He continues to guide, lead, and reassure Moses, and He explains why He is offering this guidance and reassurance:

    o   vs. 5, *"I have heard…"*

    o   vs. 5, *"I have remembered my covenant…"*

    o   vs. 7, *"Then you will know that I am the Lord your God, who brought you out from under the yoke of the Egyptians."*

- There will be no question who the deliverance comes from. It will be so obvious that the only way deliverance comes is through God's hand. For His glory.

List every way you can find in this passage to show that you see God's hand at work:

How does that challenge, comfort, encourage, or motivate you?

Exodus 6:9:

- Discouragement is debilitating and can close our hearts, minds, and ears to hear God or even understand what is reasonable.

Remember a time in the past {or maybe even right now} where you have been discouraged. List some of the things you were feeling and believing.

How could it help you in one of those moments to remember Philippians 4:8 and focus on things that are true, good, and honorable?

What are some ways you can overcome discouragement? Do you see discouragement as a choice or a burden?

Exodus 6:10-11:

- Moses seems insecure and hesitating as he continues to question God. How often do you do that? Are you quick to over think, over analyze, and get overwhelmed? These things can highlight our insecurity and hesitation in obeying God wholeheartedly, can't they?

- What does it say about you and the posture of your heart when you are questioning God or when you are insecure in something you believe He has called you to do?

What are some alternative responses that you could choose instead? How would that affect the state of your heart and your willingness to obey?

Exodus 7:1-5:

- Practice looking for slow in this set of verses. Where do you see the following:

    o Surrender:

    o Listening:

    o Obedience:

    o Worship:

Exodus 7:6:

- *"Moses and Aaron did just as the Lord commanded them."* May that be said of us as well.

Insert your name and make it your prayer.

" _____ *did just as the Lord commanded her."*

Exodus 7:7-13:

- We don't have to worry about how others will respond to or question our desire to slow. They don't have to ever understand. If God is calling our heart, we respond. God knew Pharaoh would mock them and harden his heart against God. Everything happened just as God knew it would.

How much does what others think affect your decisions?

Is there something there that needs to change?

Do you find comfort in the fact that things will turn out just as God already knows and plans?

How do you find yourself over-complicating things sometimes? It is very simple to listen, obey, and respond to God, yet we make it difficult. Why do you think that is?

Exodus 7:14-8:7:

- In the verses that follow, we will see repeated instances of slow vs. hard {hard heart, arrogance, etc.}. Slow is not something that we receive and naturally live in; it will be a repeated choice, posture, attitude, and lifestyle. We see it displayed here, where Moses was asked to obey and act time after time and God told him in advance that Pharaoh would harden his heart.

List things you see in this passage that display both slow and hardness of heart.

Slow Heart	Hard Heart

Exodus 8:8-15:

• When desperate, Pharaoh called Moses and asked him to pray for relief. Moses did, and God answered; but when relief came, Pharaoh hardened his heart again and rejected the idea of surrendering to God. This temporary surrender does not display a true heart for God.

Have you ever called out to God in a moment of desperation but not been truly surrendered to Him?

In moments of desperation, it is easy to turn to God. Do we turn to Him in the ordinary parts of life as well? Do we seek to please God in all things? And do all things for His glory? Ponder this in your heart and before God.

Exodus 8:16-22:

- God's timing may seem slow to us or even ridiculous, but remember that His goal is His glory! Now the fruit is beginning to bud on the tree; the magicians are admitting a surrender that these signs and wonders are God's doing.

Describe a time you've struggled with God's timing.

Can you look back on that time and see how God was at work now that you are on the other side of that? Praise Him for that right now, would you? Ask Him to remind you of this when you are in the midst of another circumstance where the timing doesn't match what you would prefer.

Exodus 8:23-9:12:

- There should be something distinct about us as we follow God this way. See vs. 23.

Can others around you tell something is different just by the way you follow God?

Will the way I act cause others to want to know and follow God as well? Make this a prayer of your heart.

Exodus 9:13:

- I love the words of God here to Moses to get up early in the morning and go to Pharaoh. It jumped out at me that Moses was to act first thing without delay. Getting up early and listening to God's plan has been a blessing in my days. Get started on the work that is waiting right away!

Consider why you may or may not get up early. Do you get the hard things out of the way first? If God laid something on your heart in the night, do you act upon it right away without delay? Why/why not?

Exodus 9:14-28:

- You cannot half-heartedly choose surrender. God is not fooled.

Have you ever tried to justify your lack of surrender to God?

How has God responded to that?

Exodus 9:29-35:

- Do not be tricked by false interest. Listen to GOD, not the voices of those who do not know Him.

Whose voice are you listening to most? What are the most influential voices in your life right now?

Is God pleased with your honest answer above, or do you need to make some changes?

Exodus 10:1-2:

- How we respond to this call will set an example for our children and give us an opportunity to invest in their hearts for God's glory!

What kind of example are you setting for children in your life?

Is God laying anything on your heart in relation to that?

What kind of example was set for you in slowing? If you had a good model, consider taking a few minutes to let them know!

Exodus 10:3:

- Just as we can offer to share our faith, we can offer to share what we have learned or our experience with slow. But just as we don't want to force our faith on others, we don't want to force someone to receive anything we are offering. Moses and Aaron were faithful in the calling that God laid on their hearts and to obey what He asked them to do. But they did not go to Pharaoh and scream at him or run at him trying to coerce him into giving in. They were quietly faithful and left the rest up to God.

What do you think of that last sentence?

How can you apply that to your own life?

Exodus 10:4-15:

- When we refuse God's way and do not choose a posture of humility before God, chaos, true chaos, will follow us. We think we have chaos in our day to day lives, and we do to a degree, but imagine how exponentially our chaos would grow if it were the result of rejecting God. Even Pharaoh's officials have had enough. They are in Pharaoh's face thinking, "Can't you see what is going on here?" In some ways, I love how many chances God is giving Pharaoh and the Egyptians to surrender to Him.

When have you experienced chaos from choosing not to follow God's way?

When have you experienced peace from choosing to follow God's way?

Thank God for the blessings of both lessons learned.

Exodus 10:16-20:

• Surrender must not be temporary or it is not a lasting and true change of heart.

Why do you think surrender has to be all or nothing?

Look up the word *surrender* and see if that sheds any light on what you think about this concept.

Exodus 10:21-11:10:

• These scenes unfolding are a beautiful picture of God being slow to anger. He is giving Pharaoh opportunity after opportunity to repent and choose a better way. Another picture this brings to mind is that His yoke is easy and His burden is light. Pharaoh's burden is unbearable because of his sin.

How is the fact that God is slow to anger a comfort to you?

How have you experienced the beauty and blessing of the fact that God is slow to anger?

How can you pass that blessing on to others around you?

Exodus 12:1-28:

- This reminds me that God can make a way when the way before us looks impossible. When we are walking in obedience before Him and with the posture of a slow heart, we are in the best place we could ever possibly be: resting in the center of His will. Notice verse 27, *"Then the people bowed down and worshiped."* They had the perfect Slow Day: they surrendered, listened to God, obeyed, and worshiped.

In seeing how God provided for His people, how are you encouraged? How are you challenged by their faith?

Put yourself in the Israelites' shoes and try to imagine some of the things they were thinking and feeling during this time. Write a few thoughts below.

Exodus 12:29-42:

- God will always win whether we choose to follow His plan or not. God's timing is always right, but it is not always slow and restful. This was a very intense season. The people were learning new things and obeying in new ways. They did not have time to prepare bread with yeast, so they brought unleavened bread. It is interesting to note that they were not to save any meat until morning. As much as I like to work ahead and plan ahead, that takes a measure of faith away from the current day.

- Look in verses 35-36 at the creative ways God provided for His people.

- In verse 41, notice that God brought them out on the *exact day* that marked another year in Egypt. They lived in Egypt 430 years. Not all of those years were slavery and misery, though. Similarly, we may walk a path in rightness for a period of time and then find God is leading us in a new direction.

- Verse 42 points us back to God, reminding us to worship.

What are some of the ways you have to rely on God to make it through the days He has called you to?

What are some of the creative ways God has provided for you?

How can you worship Him in and through these circumstances today?

Exodus 34:1-11

How does Moses display a slow posture? Look for surrender, listening, obedience, and worship.

God uses the word *slow* in verse 6. How does that comfort you?

Remember how the Israelites even came to need a second set of tablets? Look at Exodus 32:1-6 and 15-20. Does that add any appreciation to your heart and mind for God's slowness to anger?

What can you apply in your own life here for becoming slow to anger? Do you believe the best about people? Do you stand shoulder to shoulder? Do you talk to and not about them?[5] If you have chosen a heartstyle of slow, how will that slow your anger tendencies?

Pray along with Moses in verse 8 and personalize it:

"O Lord, if I have found favor in Your eyes, please go with me. Although I am stiff necked, forgive my wickedness and my sin, and take me as Your inheritance."

Look at verse 10 and think about God's words to *"do wonders never before done..."* Remember, who is God talking to?

---

[5] These questions are based on the Relational Covenant presented at a staff devotion at Glen Eyrie Conference Center by Jack McQueeney, Colorado Springs, CO. The Relational Covenant is: Believe the best, talk to and not about and stand shoulder to shoulder. Applying these three will help keep our relationships with one another clear before God and man.

Name some of the wonders already seen by the people:

Exodus 7:10	
Exodus 7:20-21	
Exodus 8:6	
Exodus 8:17	
Exodus 8:24	
Exodus 9:6	
Exodus 9:10	
Exodus 9:23-24	
Exodus 10:13-15	
Exodus 10:22-23	
Exodus 12:29	
Exodus 14:19-20	
Exodus 14:21-22	
Exodus 14:24	
Exodus 14:27-28	
Exodus 14:29	
Exodus 15:25	

Now read verse 10 again. What an amazing thought!

How do you see God calling the people to a heart of slow in this passage?

Numbers 14:1-24

Why are the Israelites grumbling and complaining?

Discouragement and fear has a way of crippling our view. Read verse 3. What were the people fixated on?

Read verses 3-4. They were so discouraged, they were willing and even wanting to go where?

Take a minute to remember where they came from and where they say they want to return. Recall every detail you can about what their lives were like there.

After this temper tantrum, God's presence comes to the Tent of Meeting. Read verses 10-12. What is His response?

In verses 13-19, Moses's heart knows the true nature of God and is concerned for how this will affect his reputation. What do you think about that?

What are the four things Moses lists in verse 14 that the Egyptians have observed about God?

In verses 15-16, what response does Moses fear?

Moses quotes Exodus 34:6, which we've already looked at and studied. Write Numbers 14:18a below.

What is Moses asking God for in verses 17-19?

I love verse 20. God says, "*I have* _____ _____."

It doesn't mean there are no consequences, though. The Israelites were not content with any form of slow:

- They were not surrendered to God.

- They did not listen to Him or seek less of their own agenda and more of His.

- They were not obeying.

- They did not have hearts of worship.

However, they were about to be physically slowed for many years. Let's look at some of their consequences:

Verse 23	
Verse 28	
Verse 29	
Verse 30	
Verse 33	
Verse 34	
Verse 35	

There was one beautiful exception. Look at verse 24. Who does God single out and why?

How does his ending to this story look different?

Thank You, Lord, for being slow to anger with me. I will choose surrender, listen, obey, and worship You, Lord. I want to be like Caleb and serve you wholeheartedly. And to have it said of me that I have a *different spirit* that shines for You, Lord.

Deuteronomy 7:10

In this verse, we see a contrast to God's willingness to be slow to anger toward those who love Him. When we look at the opposite, we can see how hopeless life can look to one who chooses to reject Christ. What a sad image this picture brings to mind.

Friend, the difference between being slow or quick to anger is your eternal address. Do you have Jesus as your Savior? If not, my heart reaches out to you. Would you please take that first step toward Christ? You can find out more by visiting Appendix A, talking to a trusted friend, and opening your heart to Jesus and trusting Him with your future.

If you've already settled your salvation, consider someone you know who is not on the right side of salvation. Pray for them and reach out to them; it makes an eternal difference. Ponder what life looks and feels like to one who rejects Christ. Thank Him for how He has saved you and ask Him for an opportunity to share with someone else.

Deuteronomy 23:21

While advocating a slow heart and slower pace of life to enjoy the blessings God has placed in our lives, there is a time where slowness is discouraged. When God has called us to action, slow shows a lack of faith and trust in Him. Really, this is the pulse of choosing a slow heart—that we will be surrendered to His will and not dragging our feet kicking and screaming on our way to surrender. When we delay or slowly keep our word to God, we sin and choose a way that is opposite of God's way.

Can you think of anything you have been slow to obey in? Slow to keep your word? Is there one thing you can do today to take a step toward correcting this?

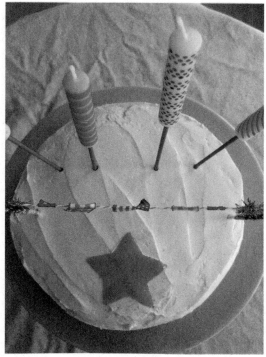

2 Kings 4:8-37

The word *slow* makes an appearance in verse 24, but when studying God's word it is good to read the context, so let's go back to verse 8. In reading these verses, there are some beautiful slow moments showing both physical slowness and a spiritually slow postured heart.

When you read verse 8, what thoughts enter your mind as you consider how both your heart and life choose slow?

Extending hospitality, serving, and making time for people all require slowing. What a beautiful picture to see this woman want to bless and serve Elisha. She was willing to set aside her agenda to include him for a meal. I can't help but think of the spontaneity that was likely involved.

There was no call, text, or email ahead that Elisha was on his way. Did he just stop in? Put yourself in the Shunammite's place. How would you respond? Be honest and realistic!

Now consider opportunities that present themselves to you for hospitality. How does hospitality require you to slow? Do you welcome or dread that? Why?

Do you think God would like to expand your thinking on hospitality? Talk to Him about it!

Continuing in verses 9-10, this sweet woman takes things a step further and desires a place for Elisha to slow. She obviously wants him to feel like he's at home. Can you imagine what a comfort that would be to one who traveled and relied on flexible accommodations wherever he went?

I love how she comes to her husband and presents her idea. I'm an idea person, so I can completely relate with this, and it has turned into somewhat of a joke, with not only my husband, but parents also, for me to say, *"I have an idea!"*

Here's something to consider: having an idea is great, but do you act on your ideas? This woman did! She got right to work and made it happen. Idea people are great; idea plus action people get things done. She's my kind of girl.

Her own heart is beautifully slow toward God, and she wants to be useful to Him. When this idea comes that she can serve one of His servants with what she's been given, she's all over it! I love it.

How can your actions bring a slow blessing in the life of another? How can you create some slow for someone else even for a few minutes during a difficult season? We certainly cannot always fix the hardships in the lives of those around us, but can we lighten their load? Process that in the space below.

Now read verses 11-13. Elisha is enjoying the fruit of her labor and generosity and wants to know what he can do for her. She displays a truly humble and serving heart. She is not seeking blessing for herself, and her answer displays true contentment with where she is in life. Her spirit is at peace. Look at the slow beauty of her mother's heart. She dared not even ask for something so big as motherhood. Remember the cultural shame in barrenness. And we know her husband is old, so perhaps it is a dream she had given up or pushed so deep she couldn't crack the door to that possibility now.

While Elisha may admire her servant heart and humble attitude, he isn't really satisfied with the idea that there is nothing he can do to encourage her heart. He and his servant have a pow-wow and think of the perfect gift for her—a son. Keep reading in verses 14-20.

But God. I have heard that phrase over and over in recent days, and it is so fitting. Things are impossible: she is barren; her husband is old. The end, right? *But God* chose to bless this home with a beautiful gift: a son.

I love the picture of the father instructing the ailing child to be delivered to his mama. There is no one like mama when a sickness or injury strikes. And we already know her beautiful heart, so we can only imagine what a loving mother she was. Her little one was laid in her lap, and she sat there *"until noon."*

She slowed. She sat and held her baby. Is it safe to imagine she was pleading to God to spare this little soul? Even so, the sick child dies in his mama's arms. Can you even imagine the loss this brings? It is a surrender like no other and one we would not choose, but it was one that she was called into.

Have you been called into surrender you did not choose? Talk to God honestly about it. He loves hearing your voice and delights in you so much.

Can you relate to the picture of slowing in the midst of chaos and tragic circumstances? When did you choose a similar slow to the one of this mama holding her baby?

As her story continues to unfold in verses 21-18, I marvel at her presence of mind to get up and go, to display this kind of faith in such a despairing time. She doesn't let on about her troubles to everyone she talks to either. Oh, how often I do just the opposite!

There is such amazing power of presence and place. She goes to Elisha's room to find Elisha himself. Is there a place or person that you seek out in times of really needing to hear from God? Describe why that place and/or that person are meaningful to you in your journey to God's heart.

She displays amazing self-control as we see her approach Elisha, and he immediately questions if everything is all right. Look at her answer initially where she says, *"Everything is all right."* She does pour out her heart in a few more verses, but this just speaks so loudly to me of the posture of her heart. God is at work in and through her, and there can be no other explanation for how she responds in difficulty.

You can continue on past verse 28 to see how God works a miracle in her life. But as you think back over the verses we just read together, consider how the Shunammite woman displays and models the following:

Surrender:

Listening:

Obedience:

Worship:

What speaks most clearly to you about her story of slowing? Why?

Finally, notice the use of the word *slow* in verse 24. It's actually a command *not* to slow down in their haste to find Elisha. I hope you are blessed by the beautiful vision of this woman's heart. What grabs your attention and causes you to want to slow down? Serve? Show people they are important? Listen to God and act on the ideas He has given you?

Nehemiah 9:1-37

Join me in reading the first three verses of Nehemiah chapter 9. Are you starting to notice the slowing? Look at how long they read God's Word and then spent in confession and worship! Beautifully slow and in choosing the right priorities, too.

When you get to verses 5-15, notice how full of praise, glory, blessing, and honor to God the people are. Write a paragraph of praise to God!

As we move ahead to verses 16-37, we get a history lesson on the Israelites' ancestors and their legacy of discontentment. Ouch. Amidst all of this, they still praise and acknowledge the truth of who God really is. We can see again and again that God is slow to anger and slow to lose patience with us.

Take a look and observe the behavior of the people vs. the response of God.

Verse	Israelite's Behavior	God's Response
16-17	Disobeyed Refused to listen Failed to remember Stiff-necked Wanted their own way	Forgiving Gracious Compassionate Slow to anger Abounding in love Faithful
18-25		
26-27a		
27b		
28a		
28b		
29		
30-31		
32-35		

Describe a time you have experienced behavior like this in yourself or in your home.

The day before I studied this passage, we maintained a family tradition to hold a little spring party in our home. We like to dye eggs, do an egg hunt, and read a couple of books on a separate day from Easter Sunday. We had spent all morning in our fun activities, and as lunchtime approached, one of my children asked, *"What is for lunch?"*

"Probably leftovers," I responded.

To this I received a very ungrateful response as if leftovers were not "fun" or "special" enough for our celebratory day. I was not exactly slow to anger or gracious in patience.

You've been here, right? It immediately takes the wind out of your sails, and it made me wish I had not been so generous in planning such a fun morning for this child who responded like this. Yet isn't that just like the Israelites? And me? I'm so thankful God doesn't treat me as my behavior merits!

Stop and thank God for how He has been slow to anger with you, generous with you, patient with you, and faithful to you.

One more story before we continue on, and it reminds me to be grateful for the times that things don't slow the way I wish they would. I can be grateful for the lessons He wants to teach my children and me in the midst, and I can be grateful that He cares enough about our hearts to invest in us this way. Also, it affirms that God wants what is best for us; He does not send trials just to torture us. He delights in good things, but as illustrated above, we can become ungrateful and huff away thinking it wasn't good enough.

One night while walking into church for the girls to sing in choir, we were toting 3 1/2 gallons of honey from a group order that I helped to coordinate. We were delivering honey to friends. I had two, and each of the girls had one or the half. There was a car coming through the drive, so I urged the girls forward as they were waiting for us to cross, and Emily dropped her gallon of honey. It broke open near the handle and began oozing out onto the pavement.

I am not going to try and put on some super mom front with you--I was upset and even shaking for the next two hours. I reminded her it was not our honey and it was not cheap. And why oh why did she do that? It was not pretty in any way.

Bless a dad walking through the parking lot who saw our predicament. He found a couple of plastic bags and loaded that gooey jug up into those bags and figured out how to lay it on its side so it would not continue leaking out. I sent the girls on their way to choir and made a couple of trips to the church, the car, and the bathroom to wash my hands and clean up.

On my way home, it struck me that I had been looking forward to when they came home from choir so I could begin our Journey Through the Holy Days {Easter season study that I posted on my blog several years ago}, so we could worship and have repentance on our minds and tongues and in our hearts.

And while I was feeling defeated and how-can-I-manage-one-more-thing-like-this kinds of feelings, God revealed a beautiful lesson for my littles and for me.

We are broken, just like that jug of honey. Our sin is oozing out all over and causing a big, sticky, broken, ugly, wasteful, icky mess. God scoops us up and makes something whole and beautiful out of us even though we don't deserve it.

I saw how the broken jug of honey shows us why we need Him, and that is exactly what this forty days before Easter is for, to remember our need for a Savior. We sin. We mess up. We need saving.

Earlier in the day, I had made a carrot cake, and we didn't have time to enjoy it after dinner. I sliced a small piece for each little to demonstrate part of our lesson. Samuel was on dessert restriction, and by the way, when do we ever *deserve* dessert? When I am steaming mad and two of three are in deep hot water, isn't this the wrong time to serve cake at bedtime?

But here is the message I was hearing in my heart: we don't deserve the cake, we don't deserve saving. It is a beautiful picture of why we were celebrating at Easter at all—a time to remember, reflect, and repent.

Just because we're all curious how stories end up, I'll tell you that I brought the sticky mess home and poured it out into mason jars. Out of the 16 cups in a gallon, a little over 2 cups was missing, which was not too bad. We swapped one of our gallons out to make it right for our friend, and I think we all walked away with a renewed perspective.

I prayed that every time I reached in to take one of those jars out of the cabinet, I would remember how much I need Jesus and what a precious gift He has given in saving me.

Are you with me? Share your thankfulness with your sweet Savior right now.

Psalm 86

Using the letters s, l, o, w, label any instances you see in this Psalm of surrender, listening, obedience, and worship. Use it as an opportunity to put yourself in each of those places and consider how your life lives out a heart of slow before God.

"Hear, O Lord, and answer me,

for I am poor and needy.

Guard my life, for I am devoted to you.

You are my God; save your servant

who trusts in you.

Have mercy on me, O Lord,

for I call to you all day long.

Bring joy to your servant,

for to you, O Lord,

I lift up my soul.

You are forgiving and good, O Lord,

abounding in love to all who call to you.

Hear my prayer, O Lord;

listen to my cry for mercy.

In the day of my trouble I will call to you,

for you will answer me.

Among the gods there is none like you, O Lord;

no deeds can compare with yours.

All the nations you have made

will come and worship before you, O Lord;

they will bring glory to your name.

For you are great and do marvelous deeds;

you alone are God.

Teach me your way, O Lord,

and I will walk in your truth;

give me an undivided heart,

that I may fear your name.

I will praise you, O Lord my God, with all my heart;

I will glorify your name forever.

For great is your love toward me;

you have delivered me from the depths of the grave.

The arrogant are attacking me, O God;

A band of ruthless men seeks my life —

men without regard for you.

But you, O Lord, are a compassionate and gracious God,

slow to anger, abounding in love and faithfulness.

Turn to me and have mercy on me;

grant your strength to your servant

and save the son of your maidservant.

Give me a sign of your goodness,

that my enemies may see it and be put to shame,

for you, O Lord, have helped me and comforted me."

Psalm 103:8

This Psalm is another reminder of God's slow to anger love for us and is a beautiful picture of praise and worship. Notice in verse 7 that Moses is mentioned here and let it bring back to your mind things we have already studied about him earlier. Write out verse 8.

Pray through this Psalm, offering the words as your own praise and worship to God. Then, write your own prayer of praise and worship to God below.

Psalm 145:8

Here is another really beautiful opportunity for worship. Take a few minutes and list all the words that describe God's character and our response:

Exalt			
Worthy			
Wonderful			
Celebrate			

Do you know what all of those words really mean? Pick two or three and find out! Look up these words in a dictionary and write out their definitions. Does this bring any new understanding to mind about worship or praising God?

Joel 2:13

After you read this verse, consider what you think the difference is between an external surrender {torn garments} and an internal surrender {your heart}.

How does it encourage you that:

-   God is slow to anger?

-   God is gracious, compassionate, and abounding in love?

-   God withholds sending calamity as He chooses?

Jonah

Buckle up, friends. This is a bumpy ride looking at the life of Jonah. It will be a longer section of Scripture to look at, and we will see what happens when we are slow to obey God and don't obey wholeheartedly.

Start by just reading the first two verses of the book {Jonah 1:1-2} and notice some things.

Who did Jonah work for full time?

What did God ask Jonah to do?

Pull out a map or flip to the back of your Bible and look up how far Nineveh was from Israel. It's not just right around the corner, is it? Now consider this: God mentions that Nineveh was known for its wickedness. Turn for a minute to the book of Nahum. Look up the references and make a note of what you learn about Nineveh in the following verses.

Nahum 1:9	They plot against God
Nahum 1:11	
Nahum 1:12	
Nahum 1:14	
Nahum 3:1	
Nahum 3:2	
Nahum 3:3	

I think you probably get the point: Assyria was not exactly a nice place to be! Take on the role of a historian for a few minutes and look up Assyria. Make note of a few interesting things you learn about their culture.

Now here is where things start to get really interesting or dicey {as my sister loves to say!}. Go back to Jonah chapter one and read verse 3.

How did Jonah respond to God?

Put yourself in Jonah's place. Would you have responded any differently?

Jonah's heart was the opposite of slow: he was not surrendered, he did not listen, he disobeyed, and he was far from worshipping God. He hurried in the other direction. Look at your map again and note where all the places mentioned are: Nineveh, Joppa, Tarshish. Do you notice anything just from looking at a map?

It's really no secret why Jonah got on that ship. Note the end of verse 3:

"After paying the fare, he went aboard and sailed for Tarshish to _____ _____ _____."

Oh my goodness, can you relate? Do you try to justify your disobedience with all kinds of reasons why it is not a good choice? I mean, we could probably help Jonah out a little bit with thoughts like:

- It's too dangerous to go to Nineveh.

- It's too far; it would take too long.

- I don't know anyone in Nineveh.

- I don't really *want* to go to Nineveh, and so on...

Keep reading and look at verse 4. Just as we saw with Moses, when we observe disobedience and rejection of God, we are seeing God's action. God doesn't want Jonah {or us} to be outside of His will. This wasn't as devastating to a large number of people as a plague was but must have been pretty scary in that the boat threatened to come apart! What did God send? Put yourself there for a minute and imagine you are out at sea. Picture some of the things you are experiencing.

Read Jonah 1:5-6. Jonah held life-changing answers and eternity-changing knowledge inside of him and where was he? ASLEEP!

When there is something in my heart that is not right or God is dealing with me on something, I do not sleep well. I am completely amazed that Jonah was in such a deep sleep! Apparently the captain was a little surprised too, because he came and asked Jonah to *"get up and _____ _____ _____ _____."*

Just think about that for a minute. In verse 5, we saw that each one called out to *"his own god,"* so there was obviously more than one possibility involved here, which means at least some did not know the One True God but false gods. It may not be a false god or idol, but is there something or someone you put false hope in during times of crisis?

It also makes me wonder if the captain noticed something different about Jonah or if he was just asking Jonah to do what all the rest of them had already been doing. This captain is searching and is about to encounter God with a big G in an amazing way. He is looking for a god who will "notice" and save them.

Read verse 7. I find it curious that they wanted to cast lots to find out who was responsible for this mess. The first thing this tells me is that this storm was big enough and sudden enough that they thought there was a bigger strength, a bigger power, behind it. They also seemed convinced that one person was responsible.

Put yourself in Jonah's place again. What was he thinking? Feeling? Do you think he was able to pray? How did he manage to keep his mouth shut while they cast lots?

And, oh boy, the lot falls on Jonah. Gulp. Now a barrage of questions comes at Jonah in verses 8-10. List any detail you see that Jonah shared with these men as the boat is being tossed by the furious storm:

- Hebrew

-

-

Jonah's life is a completely chaotic scene right now {verses 11-12}, but he has not been willing to surrender to God's will yet. The sailors ask him what to do, and while this could be a major turning point for Jonah, he is still stubbornly hanging on to avoiding Nineveh. Think of a scenario he could have suggested that would have showed a slow heart.

Can you relate to Jonah? Why or why not? How can you thank God in either case?

Read verses 13-14. This group of sailors has gained a healthy fear of God, but it isn't really from anything Jonah has said or done. Rather, it is because they know He is causing the storm. So now Jonah has royally messed up two opportunities to share God: first in refusing to go to Nineveh and now in not taking the opportunity to make a good choice in front of these sailors.

Watch this progression of their understanding of God and notice the differences:

Verse 5, *"Each cried out to his own _____."*

Verse 6, *"Pray to your _____."*

Verse 14, *"Then they cried to the _____."*

They tried to get Jonah back to land but could not because of the fierceness of the storm. Describe some of the storm possibly going on inside of Jonah.

Now we run into the first real prayer of the whole event thus far: the sailors acknowledge God's control and plead for His mercy in tossing Jonah over. What happened as soon as Jonah was overboard?

Take this thought and ponder it as a picture for your own life. How does the raging storm inside of you grow calm when you toss sin overboard and head straight for Jesus?

Do not grow weary in studying Jonah. God is not finished with him yet, and neither are we!

As you read verse 16, notice the beauty we see in the sailors' response to God. We learn three things they did:

_____ _____ the Lord

_____ _____ to the Lord

_____ _____ to Him

Meanwhile, in verse 17 we remember that Jonah is in the sea. I wonder things about him like, was he afraid? Did he try to swim/struggle? How long before the fish came?

There are a number of mind-boggling things about this scenario:

- He did not drown.

- The fish swallowed him whole.

- Creation obeys God.

- Even though Jonah's heart was hard, God still cared for him.

- Was he bewildered inside the whale?

- Imagine the darkness inside of the whale.

Plus all that time to think – ack! If I weren't a mess already, that would do me in. Getting out of the storm was one thing, but did Jonah even imagine a way out of the fish? Did he consider trying to escape? Did he fear digestion?

Do you notice anything significant about his timing inside the whale? Look at verse 17 again, *"And Jonah was inside the fish _____ _____ and _____ _____."*

Take a deep breath. I think we are at the low point. How can things get any worse? Wouldn't you rather be in the center of God's will and know without a doubt that God will take care of you than to be outside of His will, which is a much scarier place to be?

Let out that deep breath and read Jonah 2:1-9. Finally we see Jonah respond to God positively rather than running away. How does Jonah respond?

Let that sink in. Perhaps he prayed before this, but it seems important that this is the first prayer of Jonah mentioned.

Where was Jonah when he prayed?

Why is it important to note to WHOM he prayed?

I don't see Jonah *asking* for anything here. Notice the tone of his prayer, which looks similar to a Psalm. Note all the references to God:

Jonah 2:2	He answered me
2:2	You listened to my cry
2:3	

2:3	
2:4	
2:6	
2:7	
2:7	
2:9	
2:9	

Is there one of these things that stands out to you above the others? For me it was, "*When my life was ebbing away, I remembered You, Lord.*"

Did Jonah ever FORGET God? Probably not, but he did lose sight of his perspective, he did lose faith, trust, and a slow heart.

Practice thanksgiving like Jonah did. What can you find from his story so far to be thankful for?

Now apply that to your own life. Pick the hardest situation you are in right now. Can you find things to be thankful for?

Get ready. The action is going to pick back up big time. Read verse 10 and notice how God responds. How does this give you hope for seeing how God hears our prayers and responds to a soft heart and watches over and cares for us?

When you read Jonah 3:1-2, you will notice that Jonah's assignment is re-issued and has not changed, but Jonah's response has. Look at the contrast of Jonah's responses:

Jonah 1:3, *"But Jonah _____ _____from the Lord."*

Jonah 3:3, *"Jonah _____ the word of the Lord and went to Nineveh."*

Part of us is groaning, oh Jonah, look at all the trouble you could have spared yourself. But in another light, look at how much Jonah learned about God and his relationship with Him during this experience. It was life changing, and Jonah would never forget it.

Three chapters later, Jonah is arriving in Nineveh. He enters Nineveh and shares the message God has provided. {verses 4-5}

How is his message received?

The people did at least three things in response. Look in verse 5 to find them:

1. They believed God.

2.

3.

Take a minute to look back over your list of things we learned about the Ninevites. Does their response startle you in light of their reputation?

If that startles you, just wait! The king is about to catch wind of what is going on. List the actions involved in the king's response from Jonah 3:6-9.

-

-

-

-

-

-

-

-

The king lowered himself by doing exactly what he was asking his people to do. They are beginning to adopt a heart attitude and posture of s.l.o.w.

Now look at God's response in Jonah 3:10, "*He had _____ and _____ bring the destruction He had promised.*"

What does that do to your heart? How does it encourage or comfort you?

Starting in chapter 4, Jonah's response is surprising and difficult. What was his attitude after God withheld destruction from the Ninevites? Read Jonah 4:1-4.

I find it interesting that right after we learn his state of mind and response, *he prays*. But it is more of a tirade than a prayer. Can you relate? Have you ever felt angry at God's mercy or compassion? Jonah went so far as to say that life wasn't worth living anymore. He recognized God's character accurately, but he resented it. Process that for a minute and record any thoughts here.

Look at verse 4 again. God asks Jonah a question. Write it out below.

Jonah's answer is not recorded for us, but by his behavior I would speculate that he thinks he has a right to be angry. So Jonah huffs off and plops down to get comfy, waiting to relish the sight of Nineveh's destruction. It strikes me as difficult to understand Jonah. God has led him and protected him so powerfully. How could he forget so easily? How could he treat God so poorly? He does not have a true heart of slow. He may have chosen slow tendencies on occasion, but it has not become a way of life or the heart. Jonah has not really allowed this life-changing experience to change him. At least not for the better.

Notice Jonah 3:6-8. The word *provided* appears three times. What three things did God provide:

1.

2.

3.

Just for fun, draw a happy or a sad face next to each one to indicate how Jonah would have responded. What made Jonah happy? His own comfort, right? He didn't *need* to be sitting there; that was his choice.

Now name some ways God provides for you!

Jonah allowed his outer circumstances to dictate his feelings. How is that dangerous? Where do you see yourself in that practice?

In the last few verses of Jonah 4:8-11 there is a conversation between Jonah and God. It is really an embarrassment for Jonah that this is remembered for all time. If you were writing an account of your life, can you relate to Jonah's exposure of himself?

It is somewhat easy to look at Jonah's childish behavior and almost laugh at his drama and foolishness, but I think we can honestly look at our own hearts and realize we do not always respond righteously. Peek back at verses 8-9 one more time. Imagine Jonah's tone of voice, body language, posture, and facial expression.

What do you think caused Jonah to make the bold statement he uses in verse 8?

Look at God's response in verse 9. Our society tends to have such an "I deserve" mentality or "it's my right to be angry at God." At this moment, it feels like we are far from slow. The train has sort of derailed, and we are not left with a neat and tidy ending. I hope you will see, though, the chaos that fills and follows a heart not committed to choosing a slow heart before God. It does not look appealing and does not faithfully serve God or our own best interests. What a mess!

Let's finish off this section on Jonah. Jonah feels it is his right to be angry, even angry enough to die. When a child responds stubbornly like this, they are usually looking for you to make some concession to their bold demand. What could Jonah's intention have been? Spoiled? Wanting God to change His mind? Feeling guilty? Lack of contentment and peace in his own heart, mind, and life? Honestly, it is amazing that God doesn't just zap him right then and there.

How does God respond instead?

What if Jonah had chosen a heart of slow? Can you rewrite a possible ending to this story?

Like a misbehaving or poorly trained child, I'm ready to leave Jonah behind, but let his life lessons stick with you and hover in your heart to remind you of the soul chaos that comes from choosing a life focused on self rather than God.

Nahum 1:3

Look at verse 1. Who is this passage about?

Nineveh? Didn't we just study Nineveh and Jonah's message in depth? I noticed one very interesting thing in the introduction to each book:

- Jonah was written around the time of 785-760 BC.

- Nahum was probably written during the time of 663-612 BC.

Did you catch that? This passage is 100 years later, and it seems Nineveh has not remained changed for the long haul because we see a prophet is being sent a second time.

Read verse 2. How does God see Nineveh?

Write out verse 3a:

Verses 3-8 describe the display of God's power. List some of the ways:

- Whirlwind/storm/clouds

- Rebukes the sea and it dries

-

-

-

-

-

-

-

-

-

-

What do these things have in common? They are created things, and God is reminding us of His authority over creation. We are His creation also.

In the midst of all these reminders, He holds out a light of hope. Read verse 7 and write it out here:

What is your responsibility to receive this refuge from Him? We must TRUST. When we lose that, we are like Nineveh, trusting our own strength or thoughts.

How does it encourage or challenge you that God reminds us He is slow to anger in the midst of this trouble and judgment of Nineveh? Remember how many years this has been. How does this trust fit with a slow posture to you?

Luke 17:11-19

As I was planning my day and what I needed to get done, I thought of a few people I needed and wanted to send notes of thanks to. The phrase *slow to give thanks* came to mind as I pictured the writing and sending of a paper or electronic note.

One thing I continue to be aware of in this slowing is that people are worth slowing for. If I rush through emptying the dishwasher or work as hard and fast as I can for fifteen minutes, won't that allow me to be freer to slow for souls? To let them know they are worth slowing for?

When I think of this, Jesus comes to mind. This was His expertise while on Earth – ministry to people. He slowed for souls. But, back to the beginning thought – slow to give thanks.

Naturally, a next thought was of the ten lepers where only one came back. I would love to think that the one who returned was a slow-lover and learner like me.

The first thing I notice when reading this passage is that Jesus was traveling. Now, this train of thought is tricky because He knows and thinks differently than I do. But I can try to put myself in His shoes for a moment. If I am traveling, I have a destination and goal in mind. I wonder how I would react to a detour or interruption such as this. Would I be able or willing to slow my heart, mind, and soul to see the heart of the other and perhaps God's higher purpose?

Of course, I am not able to heal as Jesus did physically or spiritually, but if a soul calls out to me, I can point them to the One who can. Do I embrace every opportunity to glorify God as Jesus beautifully models?

Jesus did not perform a miracle visibly right there on the spot. He gave them a task to do in response to their request. This requires faith and their participation. It is not one-sided. It strikes me that when someone makes a request of me, I will likely try to carry it out to the fullest, wrap it up with a bow, and present it on a silver platter. Jesus knew when to do that, but He also knew when to restrain for the benefit of others and God's glory. This is a boundary He knows how to set. What can you learn from His example?

Picture this: as they went, they were cleansed. It was in the process of obeying and displaying of faith that their healing took place.

These ten were so close to choosing a heart posture of slow, but they chose instead a "slo" posture, leaving off the worship. Except for one! He is a beautiful picture to us! Don't you think Jesus had continued His journey? How did the leper even find Jesus? Imagine how much harder it was to find and be found when technology was not tracking us like it is these days! All the others went back to some other life, but this *one*, oh this one.

This is also a picture to us of how we may feel about choosing slow. We may feel like we are the only one pursuing this lifestyle and heart-style. But look at what blessing this one received for choosing a narrow, less-traveled road! And, he was an unlikely candidate for choosing Jesus, as the Bible notes he was a Samaritan.

Look again at verse 19, *"Rise and go your faith has made you well."* Isn't this a picture of not only his physical healing but now spiritual as well? This has changed his life forever – literally and not just for his earth-bound days.

To recap, we see the elements of a slow posture here:

- Surrender: the man called out to Jesus out of a deep need and a desperation; these were already the lowest of the low, outcasts, rejected by many. Yet they lowered themselves by admitting their need and acknowledging that He is greater.

- Listening: Jesus gave them a task and they did it; they had a responsibility to act.

- Obedience: when Jesus said "go" they went. There is no delay mentioned.

- Worship: this is where 9 out of 10 got out of the slow lane and jumped right back into the broad path of life and culture. Yet one lone soul is seeking and full of thanks, and he exuberantly comes! He throws himself at Jesus' feet; he calls out praise in a loud voice. It strikes me that as lepers they *had* to call out loudly to alert others so they could stay away. This one is so accustomed to this loud speaking and how it turns people away in fear, but it is not so with Jesus, who allows him the freedom to come close and have the opportunity to live a quiet life.

How do you think these men lived after this? While we aren't given the details, would you tend to think that our one slow chooser will make the most eternal impact because he not only had his health restored but changed his future in eternity? Will he minister to others? Share his faith? Continue in a posture of worship and thankfulness?

More importantly, will you?

Luke 24:25

Sometimes slow is negative.

After you read this verse, you will see that Jesus reprimanded two of His disciples for their foolishness and slowness of heart in believing. They had known Jesus *personally* in the flesh and learned from Him yet still had trouble understanding and receiving what He said at face value.

In what ways are you slow of heart and foolish?

Jesus' solution was to go back to the beginning and explain, just like we often do with our children. Then, Jesus stayed with them and enjoyed a meal, and their eyes were opened. When you spend quality time with God seeking time in His presence, this opens your eyes, renews your perspective, and refocuses your attentions.

How do you need your eyes opened? Set aside some quality time to study God's Word and have your focus renewed. Oh, may we not be slow of heart and slow to believe You, Jesus.

Acts 27:7

Paul is making very slow progress by ship on a journey to Italy. He is a prisoner and winter is fast approaching.

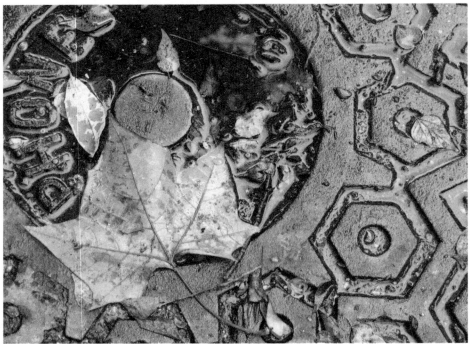

If you read the entire chapter of Acts 27, you will visualize a broader scope of what was taking place. Frequently, I will think to myself that if I am struggling to make something happen or almost forcing it, it is not likely what I should be doing. Such was the case for the crew of this ship in verses 9-20. But God holds out hope. {See vs. 21-25}

Staying close to God and not only listening to Him but also obeying Him is truly the best place for us to be: in the center of His will.

What are you seeing slow progress in? Are you seeking God and making sure you are in the center of His will? Though God may seem slow to answer, He is never late. How will you praise Him for His timing in your circumstances today?

Hebrews 5:11

Here we come face-to-face with another example of slow being used in the negative sense. Being slow to learn, not progressing from the basics.

God's Word makes it clear that those who are receiving this letter have been believers long enough that they should have grown and now be able to teach others. But they are needing to be taught basic truths, similar to what we read in Luke 24:25.

Fill in the blanks here for verse 14:

"... who by _____ _____ have _____ themselves to distinguish good and evil."

Where are you? Have you progressed from milk to meat? Is there an area where you are slow to learn?

Just like anything, we are seeing that a balance of slow is healthy. Being too slow or too hasty — neither is healthy.

James 1:19-21

I love how this verse begins – *"my dear brothers take note of this…"* It is an urging with love and sincerity to hear what is being said and not forget.

The urging is to be:

• Quick to listen

• Slow to speak

• Slow to become angry

Right there alone we can see a beautiful heart posture of slow. But how are you doing at being quick to listen? Slow to speak? Slow to become angry?

Isn't it true that by our human nature, we are slow to listen, quick to speak, and quick to become angry? We need God's nature to come in and take over.

What do you think of when you think of a good listener?

How about someone who is slow to speak?

When you think of slow to become angry, what comes to mind? Verse 20 gives us a great reason why we should be slow in anger, *"for man's anger does not bring about the righteous life that God desires."*

This is all well and good and really, it's wonderful. But in real life, how do we put this in action? What are some ways we can learn to be quick to listen, slow to speak, and slow to become angry? Here are a few thoughts that came to mind; I hope you will think this over and see what you can add to it:

- Pray! Ask for God's help.

- To be a good listener; remember that simple golden rule we have all heard before to treat others the same way you want to be treated. Try to put yourself in their place and really listen with your heart, not just your ears.

- When I am practicing being a good listener, it is another opportunity to adopt a slow posture:

    o Surrender: place another ahead of myself.

    o Listen: keep stories I have experienced to myself; don't be in a hurry to share my opinion and thoughts.

    o Obey: remember it is God I must obey and not man.

    o Worship: keep the ultimate goal in mind: to bring glory to God.

- Pick a verse or two to memorize. When you are in that moment, repeat the verse to yourself as many times as you need to.

- Don't give up when you fail. For many of us, it will take a retraining of our habits and responses. When we do fail, though, we can make it right. We can ask forgiveness and confess we are struggling and then go to God asking for help to grow and respond differently next time.

- When it is within your control, don't let things go until you reach your boiling point and explode. Learn to set healthier boundaries and keep an eye on what triggers your quick reactions. If we set boundaries earlier, perhaps the situation will not escalate to boiling level.

- Stop and take a deep breath and pray; consider if this is a battle worth fighting.

- Romans 12:17-18, *"Do not repay anyone evil for evil. Be careful to do what is right in the eyes of everybody. If it is possible, as far as it depends on you, live at peace with everybody."*

- Consider mentally or even verbally walking through surrender, listen, obey, worship. You could pray something like this:

    o Lord, I surrender to You and Your will. I want less of me in this and more of You. I want to hear and obey Your Word. I want to bring You glory and worship and praise You for who You are. Help me right now to keep my calm and handle this in a way that pleases You. Amen.

- Find something to be thankful for and spend time thinking on that instead.

- Remember Philippians 4:8, *"Finally, brothers, whatever is true, whatever is noble, whatever is right, whatever is pure, whatever is lovely, whatever is admirable – if anything is excellent or praise worthy – think about such things."*

o   Go through that list and say to yourself, Is this true? Is this noble? Is this right? If it isn't, toss it out and don't dwell on it.

What other things come to your mind?

In verse 21, we are given two actions to take. What are they?

1.

2.

The very end of the verse offers an eternal result:

Oh friend, if you have not yet received this free gift of salvation, I hope and pray you will! I've written a special note to you in Appendix A of this book.

2 Peter 3:8-9

Reading verse 8, you can hear Peter's tone as he is closing out this letter. He is urgent that this one thing is of value, and he is gentle in holding it out to them. He genuinely cares for his friends. Peter points us back to Psalm 90:4, where we are taught that our perception of time is different than time from God's perspective.

It appears there is at least one more point Peter wants to make: God's timing is always right. He is never too early or too late.

"The Lord is not slow in keeping His promises, as some understand slowness." (2 Peter 3:9a) You can look up Hebrews 10:37 for some encouragement on what this promise is. I am intrigued by the phrase, *"as some understand slowness."* What differing things can slow mean to you?

Has your view of slow changed through this study? If so, how?

Do you think God views slow the same way we do? Why or why not?

One of the original definitions for slow in the Bible includes the word *patient,* and we see it again here. How do you think slow and patient could go together, especially from God's perspective?

God even tells us the motivation for His slowness and patience. What is it? How does that encourage or challenge you?

What words or thoughts come to your mind as you let God's motive simmer?

How does the slow posture I've proposed fit in here? Jot down a few words or thoughts for each word based on these verses. Keep in mind the promise we referenced as well in Hebrews 10:37.

- Surrender:

- Listen:

- Obey:

- Worship:

More Slow Study

In closing out this word study on slow and where it appears in the Bible, please know that there is still more! There are numerous examples that Jesus set for us in slowing both spiritually and physically. Jesus was never in a hurry. If working through this extensive study has whet your appetite for more, there is SO much more available penned by the very heart of God. Try looking up any of these and looking for a heart posture of SLOW:

- Ruth {Book of Ruth}

- Hannah {1 Samuel}

- Esther {Book of Esther}

- Mary, Jesus' mother {Luke 1:26-56, Luke 2, and various other passages}

- Nehemiah {Book of Nehemiah}

- Zacchaeus {Luke 19:1-10}

- Stephen {Acts 7}

- Philip {Acts 8:26 and following}

- Ethiopian Eunuch {Acts 8:30 and following}

- Saul/Paul {Acts 9}

- King David {1 Samuel 17 and following before he becomes king; 1 Chronicles 11 and following after he becomes king}

- Daniel {Book of Daniel}

- Shadrach, Meshach, and Abednego {Daniel 3}

AFTERWORD

Dear Friend,

I want so much to know what this journey of slow has been for you! I trust it has refreshed your heart in just the ways God knew you needed. Through study, journaling and thinking through the pace of life – I hope that these words have spurred your thinking on to what slow can mean in your own life.

This is just the beginning! If you implement even one little slow change, it can snowball into more.

Thank you for picking up this book! And, thank you for beginning to interact and engage with slowing down. These actions of slowing can impact you and your families for good!

If you'd like to interact further with me, here are a few options:

Visit my blog: www.thehomespunheart.blogspot.com

Join me on Instagram: therustyrobin; tag your photos of beautifully slowing #slowlanebook

Send me an email: thehomespunheart@hotmail.com

Allow slow to become beautiful in your life!

Slowing with you,

Monica

APPENDIX A: GOD'S FREE GIFT TO YOU

Dear Friend,

I don't know how a copy of this book found its way to you, but I am so glad it did. In these pages, you've seen evidence of a life lived with and for God. I want so much for you to know that life and peace as well.

A heart without God can never truly slow, because He is the one who set the example for us in resting and He promises to give us His peace. We truly cannot gain this rest or peace any other way than through Him.

I want you to know that God created you with a special and unique purpose in His kingdom. He created you for His glory. First, you must understand that God loves you so much. He loves you enough that He sent His one and only Son, Jesus Christ, to earth to die and pay the price our sin requires.

What is sin? Sin is anything we think, say, or do that does not please God. And oh, my friend, every single one of us has things in our lives that fall into that category. The first step in receiving this free gift is to admit that you have sinned. Just confess that in your heart right now to Him. Nothing is too big or ugly to confess. He already knows and, remember, He loves you so much.

Now you must take that always hard first step of faith. Believe that Jesus died for your sins. Believe that He loves you. Believe that when you ask for forgiveness, you have received it. If you would like to receive Jesus and His precious gift into your heart, you can pray something like this prayer:

Dear Jesus, I admit I am a sinner and I have done things that do not please You. I ask for Your forgiveness and believe that You sent Your Son Jesus to die in my place. I want to live forever in heaven with You. Please come into my heart and find a welcoming place here at home in me. Thank You, God, for hearing my prayer and loving me enough to save me. In Jesus' Name, amen.

Please begin to unwrap this free gift of eternal life with our heavenly Father by talking to someone you trust who knows God. Ask God for understanding when you read His Word, and ask for wisdom and guidance in any changes you need to make in your life.

If you aren't sure what to do next, visit www.peacewithgod.net or ask a trusted friend.

Souls are the only thing we can take with us for eternity, where we will experience the ultimate surrender, listening, obedience, and worship. Oh, friend, how I hope you are there with me.

Praying for you,

Monica

APPENDIX B: DOING A WORD STUDY

If choosing a word and studying how it appears in the Bible is new to you, or if you just really happened to enjoy this method of study, here are some thoughts for you on doing your own word study on any word that God brings to mind often or places on your heart. What I am sharing here is just how I like to do a word study. I'm sure there are other ways, and you may even come up with something of your own that you like better!

When I begin a word study, it usually means I have a topic or word that has been on my heart or that I want to know more about what God's Word says on that idea/topic. I usually start by looking in a concordance {I use the Zondervan Exhaustive NIV Concordance and the Strongest NIV Exhaustive Concordance} and write down the reference of every time that word appears in Scripture. If you don't have access to a concordance, you can use any number of apps or websites to look up the same information. I've used www.biblegateway.com and www.crosswalk.com.

In my quiet times in the morning, I can work through looking those passages up and making notes about what I learn in each one. Keep an open eye for recurring words/thoughts that emerge from this, because there may be other words that support your topic that you can also look up as part of your study.

At this point, you can do whatever you want with your study. You can look up other words that have come up and compare them to your original word. You can write a definition of the word you were studying based on all the things you have learned. Share it in a blog post or quick post on Instagram or Facebook or just keep it in your journal for your own study and use.

I have really enjoyed doing word studies and learning in more detail what a certain word means in God's Word. It has helped me to shape my thinking on different things and go much more in depth in my own personal study time.

This can also be a great tool for when you are seeking God's wisdom and guidance in a particular idea or when you are dealing with a specific issue with one of your children. You could even assign a word study that you simplify by writing down only some of the references for your children or to strengthen a training idea you've been working on.

I hope this is a blessing to you in your own personal study of God's Word!

APPENDIX C – VERSE CARDS FOR STRESS MANAGEMENT PLAN

I hope you will cut these cards out and use them in any way that is a blessing to you in reducing stress and choosing peace. Some ideas include:

- Hole punch cards and thread onto a ring.

- Post cards in various places you will see them often: dashboard, over your kitchen sink or on a mirror.

- Tuck into notes you write to friends or family.

- Place cards in an envelope to refer to as needed.

- Clip to string or thread through string and create a garland of visible reminders.

---

2 Chronicles 14:7b, *"The land is still ours, because we have sought the Lord our God: we sought him and he has given us rest on every side."*

Psalm 46:10, *"Be still, and know that I am God: I will be exalted among the nations, I will be exalted in the earth."*

Monica Wilkinson

2 Chronicles 14:11, "*Then Asa called to the Lord his God and said, 'Lord, there is no one like you to help the powerless against the mighty. Help us, O Lord our God, for we rely on you, and in your name we have come against this vast army. O Lord, you are our God, do not let man prevail against you.'*"

2 Corinthians 12:8-10, "*Three times I pleaded with the Lord to take it away from me. But he said to me, 'My grace is sufficient for you, for my power is made perfect in weakness.' Therefore I will boast all the more gladly about my weaknesses, so that Christ's power may rest on me. That is why, for Christ's sake, I delight in weaknesses, in insults, in hardships, in persecutions, in difficulties. For when I am weak, then I am strong.*"

Philippians 4:13, "*I can do everything through him who gives me strength.*"

Philippians 4:19, "*And my God will meet all your needs according to his glorious riches in Christ Jesus.*"

Philippians 4:8, "*Finally, brothers, whatever is true, whatever is noble, whatever is right, whatever is pure, whatever is lovely, whatever is admirable – if anything is excellent or praiseworthy – think about such things.*"

Monica Wilkinson

Philippians 4:6-7, *"Do not be anxious about anything, but in everything, by prayer and petition, with thanksgiving, present your requests to God. And the peace of God, which transcends all understanding, will guard your hearts and your minds in Christ Jesus."*

Ephesians 6:14-17, *"Stand firm then, with the belt of truth buckled around your waist, with the breastplate of righteousness in place, and with your feet fitted with the readiness that comes from the gospel of peace. In addition to all this, take up the shield of faith, with which you can extinguish all the flaming arrows of the evil one. Take the helmet of salvation and the sword of the Spirit, which is the word of God."*

Joshua 1:9, *"Have I not commanded you? Be strong and courageous. Do not be terrified; do not be discouraged, for the Lord your God will be with you wherever you go."*

2 Chronicles 15:2b, *"The Lord is with you when you are with him. If you seek him, he will be found by you, but if you forsake him, he will forsake you."*

2 Chronicles 15:7, *"But as for you, be strong and do not give up, for your work will be rewarded."*

Monica Wilkinson

2 Chronicles 15:8a, *"When Asa heard these words and the prophecy of Azariah son of Oded the prophet, he took courage..."*

2 Chronicles 15:12, *"They entered into a covenant to seek the Lord, the God of their fathers, with all their heart and soul."*

2 Chronicles 15:15b, *"They sought God eagerly, and he was found by them. So the Lord gave them rest on every side."*

2 Chronicles 16:9a, *"For the eyes of the Lord range throughout the earth to strengthen those whose hearts are fully committed to him."*

2 Chronicles 19:11b, *"Act with courage, and may the Lord be with those who do well."*

Monica Wilkinson

2 Chronicles 20:4, *"The people of Judah came together to seek help from the Lord; indeed, they came from every town in Judah to seek him."*

2 Chronicles 20:12, *"O our God, will you not judge them? For we have no power to face this vast army that is attacking us. We do not know what to do, but our eyes are upon you."*

2 Chronicles 20:15, *"He said: 'Listen, King Jehoshaphat and all who live in Judah and Jerusalem! This is what the Lord says to you: Do not be afraid or discouraged because of this vast army. For the battle is not yours, but God's.'"*

2 Chronicles 20:17, *"You will not have to fight this battle. Take up your positions; stand firm and see the deliverance the Lord will give you, O Judah and Jerusalem. Do not be afraid; do not be discouraged. Go out to face them tomorrow, and the Lord will be with you."*

Jeremiah 33:3, *"Call to me and I will answer you and tell you great and unsearchable things you do not know."*

Monica Wilkinson

2 Chronicles 20:20, *"Early in the morning they left for the Desert of Tekoa. As they set out, Jehoshaphat stood and said, 'Listen to me, Judah and people of Jerusalem! Have faith in the Lord your God and you will be upheld; have faith in his prophets and you will be successful.'"*

2 Chronicles 20:21-22, *"After consulting the people, Jehoshaphat appointed men to sing to the Lord and to praise him for the splendor of his holiness as they went out at the head of the army, saying: 'Give thanks to the Lord for his love endures forever.' As they began to sing and praise, the Lord set ambushes against the men of Ammon and Moan and Mount Seir who were invading Judah, and they were defeated."*

Psalm 23, *"The Lord is my shepherd, I shall not be in want. He makes me lie down in green pastures, he leads me beside quiet waters, he restores my soul. He guides me in paths of righteousness for his name's sake. Even though I walk through the valley of the shadow of death, I will fear no evil, for you are with me; your rod and your staff, they comfort me. You prepare a table before me in the presence of my enemies. You anoint my head with oil; my cup overflows. Surely goodness and love will follow me all the days of my life, and I will dwell in the house of the Lord forever."*

Proverbs 31:26, *"She speaks with wisdom, and faithful instruction is on her tongue."*

Proverbs 31:30, *"Charm is deceptive, and beauty is fleeting; but a woman who fears the Lord is to be praised."*

Monica Wilkinson

1 Peter 5:7, *"Cast all your anxiety on him because he cares for you."*

Titus 2:4, *"Then they can train the younger women to love their husbands and children…"*

Psalm 27:14, *"Wait for the Lord; be strong and take heart and wait for the Lord."*

Isaiah 50:4, *"The Sovereign Lord has given me an instructed tongue, to know the word that sustains the weary. He wakens me morning by morning, wakens my ear to listen like one being taught."*

Matthew 11:28-30, *"Come to me, all you who are weary and burdened, and I will give you rest. Take my yoke upon you and learn from me, for I am gentle and humble in heart, and you will find rest for your souls. For my yoke is easy and my burden is light."*

Monica Wilkinson

Isaiah 40:11, "*He tends his flock like a shepherd: he gathers the lambs in his arms and carries them close to his heart; he gently leads those that have young.*"

Isaiah 40:28b-31, "*He will not grow tired or weary and his understanding no one can fathom. He gives strength to the weary and increases the power of the weak. Even youths grow tired and weary, and young men stumble and fall; but those who hope in the Lord will renew their strength. They will soar on wings like eagles; they will run and not grow weary, they will walk and not be faint.*"

Isaiah 41:10, "*So do not fear, for I am with you; do not be dismayed, for I am your God. I will strengthen you and help you: I will uphold you with my righteous right hand.*"

Psalm 25:4-5, "*Show me your ways, O Lord, teach me your paths; guide me in your truth and teach me, for you are God my Savior, and my hope is in you all day long.*"

Isaiah 7:4, "*Say to him, 'Be careful, keep calm and don't be afraid. Do not lose heart because of these two smoldering stubs of firewood – because of the fierce anger of Rezin and Aram and of the son of Remaliah.'*"

Monica Wilkinson

:15, *"This is what the Sovereign Lord, the Holy One of Israel, says: 'In repentance and* your salvation, in quietness and trust is your strength, but you would have none of it.'"

Isaiah 26:3, *"You will keep in perfect peace him whose mind is steadfast, because he trusts in you."*

Isaiah 26:12, *"Lord, you establish peace for us; all that we have accomplished you have done for us."*

Isaiah 30:18-21, *"Yet the Lord longs to be gracious to you; he rises to show you compassion. For the Lord is a God of justice. Blessed are all who wait for him!"*

Proverbs 3:17-18, *"Her ways are pleasant ways, and all her paths are peace. She is a tree of life to those who embrace her; those who lay hold of her will be blessed."*

Isaiah 30
rest

APPENDIX D: BEAUTIFUL SLOW AR ... ⁶

---

⁶ Artwork designed by Sarah of Printable Verses: www.etsy.com.

Isaiah 30:15, "*This is what the Sovereign Lord, the Holy One of Israel, says: 'In repentance and rest is your salvation, in quietness and trust is your strength, but you would have none of it.'*"

Isaiah 26:3, "*You will keep in perfect peace him whose mind is steadfast, because he trusts in you.*"

Isaiah 26:12, "*Lord, you establish peace for us; all that we have accomplished you have done for us.*"

Isaiah 30:18-21, "*Yet the Lord longs to be gracious to you; he rises to show you compassion. For the Lord is a God of justice. Blessed are all who wait for him!*"

Proverbs 3:17-18, "*Her ways are pleasant ways, and all her paths are peace. She is a tree of life to those who embrace her; those who lay hold of her will be blessed.*"

APPENDIX D: BEAUTIFUL SLOW ART PRINT[6]

---
[6] Artwork designed by Sarah of Printable Verses: www.etsy.com.

APPENDIX E: SLOW PRAYERS

Slow Prayer for the Stressful Day

Dear God,

This day is unraveling so fast my head is spinning. Please help me before it is completely derailed. I need You, Jesus.

I surrender this day to You. I want to listen to You, obey You, and worship You.

Please help me to rest in You today, Lord. Show me anything that can go from today. Let me literally sit still and rest. I will pause and take a deep breath and just *be*.

Turn this day around, Jesus, that I may please and glorify You with my only chance to live this day.

Let me live with no regrets. Remind me of the cost of hurry, rush, and stress and of the blessings of slow, still, and resting in You.

Thank You for the peace that only You can give. Even when I fail at slow, You are still with me and I am still loved. Thank You for second chances.

Amen

Monica Wilkinson

Prayer of Thanks for the Slow Day

Dear God,

Thank You that You are the author of slow and You modeled the first Slow Day to us Yourself. Thank You for the slow You brought to my heart and our home today. Jesus, I am grateful and at peace, resting in You.

Thank You for the ways You brought beauty to my world today {be specific}. These gifts are like little hugs from You. Thank You for speaking my love language.

Your Word feeds my soul, Jesus. And slow feeds my heart and makes me a better daughter, sister, wife, mother, and friend.

Thank You for modeling slow and teaching me Your ways.

I love and need You, Jesus. Even in my slow, may I please and glorify You.

Amen

SPECIAL THANKS:

I love to read the page of thanks in a book and see all the little pieces that contributed behind the scenes! How exciting to get to write my own now.

To each one who has encouraged me in any way during this process, I just want to hug you. You believed in this project God had laid on my heart, and no matter how big or crazy it sounded, so many of you encouraged and listened and walked alongside. I am so grateful.

Special thanks to my friends at The Bible Student – my favorite place to hang out to study and write. I had been longing for a place like this, and God provided through you.

To my mom, Ruth, and sister, Carrie, thank you for being advance readers! Where I am seriously lacking in proper grammar skills, you both make up for it in heaps, and I am so grateful. For every time you wrote, "What did you mean here?" I thank you, and for every encouragement along the way my heart was built up. I am so grateful for both of you. I love you.

To Kennisha Hill for hearing my heart and catching the vision for this book. It made me smile the first time we talked on the phone to hear your little sweets popping into your office, and knowing they were near their mama just warmed my heart.

To Amanda Bumgarner for going through this manuscript with an eagle eye – thank you for all of your editorial suggestions. Your encouragement and constructive feedback have made the finished project all the better.

To Lin Jaecks for saving the day at the eleventh hour on the layout and design for this book. Your cheerful spirit were a joy to work with and I am so grateful for your generous service!

To Amy Wilson for taking my photo shown on the back cover. You have supported and cheered from the very beginning even when the idea was just beginning and I was afraid to talk about it. You wrangled kids and cleaned up mud for those photos and most of all, you are a great friend!

To Shay and Melissa - thank you for your friendship! For listening to more details about my book, for encouraging and supporting, for being there. I am blessed.

To David, my husband, for taking the kids to Awana and choir every Sunday and Wednesday evening so I could sneak away and write/study/have quiet. Thank you for teaching me to love the phrase, "No rush," and to finally believe you when you say it. You have never doubted but always believed the best about me, especially when I don't deserve it. Thank you for working so hard so I can be home with our kids slowing and enjoying life together every day. I love you.

To Emily, Rachel, and Samuel for loving to slow with me. Our Slow Days are my favorite day every time. We make the best memories, eat yummy food, marvel over God's creation, and so much more. I love slowing with you so much and am grateful for these memories we are treasuring up together. I love being your mama.

Jesus, thank You so much for teaching me how to slow, for guiding my steps in this process, and caring tenderly for my heart. When fear threatens to overtake me, thank you for always being there. Thank you for a love of studying your Word and for what a precious gift we have when we open it and take it to heart. The desire of my heart is that anything here that blesses or encourages another heart brings You glory and praise and honor. I love you.